AFRICAN
AMERICAN
ACCULTURATION

For our families

AFRICAN AMERICAN ACCULTURATION

DECONSTRUCTING RACE AND REVIVING CULTURE

HOPE LANDRINE
ELIZABETH A. KLONOFF

SAGE Publications
International Educational and Professional Publisher
Thousand Oaks London New Delhi

For information address:

SAGE Publications, Inc.
2455 Teller Road
Thousand Oaks, California 91320
E-mail: order@sagepub.com

SAGE Publications Ltd.
6 Bonhill Street
London EC2A 4PU
United Kingdom

SAGE Publications India Pvt. Ltd.
M-32 Market
Greater Kailash I
New Delhi 110 048 India

Printed in the United States of America

Library of Congress Cataloging-in-Publication Data

Landrine, Hope, 1954-
    African American acculturation: Deconstructing race and reviving culture/authors, Hope Landrine, Elizabeth A. Klonoff.
        p.   cm.
    Includes bibliographical references and index.
    ISBN 0-8039-7282-2 (acid-free paper). — ISBN 0-8039-7283-0 (pbk.: acid-free paper)
    1. Afro-Americans—Cultural assimilation.   2. Afro-Americans—Race identity.   3. Afro-Americans—Health and hygiene.   I. Klonoff, Elizabeth A.   II. Title.
E185.625.L36   1996
305.896'073—dc20   95-41809

96 97 98 99 10 9 8 7 6 5 4 3 2 1

This book is printed on acid-free paper.

Sage Production Editor: Diana E. Axelsen

Contents

Preface

This book argues and demonstrates two points. The first (Chapter 1) is that African Americans and European Americans are not races but instead are ethnic groups, where *race* refers to genetic differences and *ethnicity* refers to cultural differences. We demonstrate through logic and through scientific evidence that race is not a scientific or genetic category but a political one. Ethnic groups are lumped together and called "Black" and "White" races, not for scientific reasons, but for purely political purposes. One of the many proofs of this is that the many ethnic groups that have been lumped together as the White race differ genetically from each other yet nonetheless are regarded as a single race. We argue and demonstrate that the time has come to reject race as a way of categorizing or understanding anyone, Black and White alike.

With the proof that African Americans are not a race but an ethnic (cultural) group in hand, we then make our second point: The best approach to understanding an ethnic group is to analyze the extent to which its members participate in their own culture versus the culture of the dominant society; the best approach is to examine their levels of acculturation. Like Asian Americans and Mexican Americans, African Americans are understood better in terms of the extent to which they are immersed in their own cultures than in terms of race or biology. We then turn to an analysis of African American culture, describe our theory of African American acculturation (Chapter 2), and then present the first acculturation scale ever developed for African Americans (Chapter 3). We follow this with preliminary scientific investigations (Chapters 4 and 5) in which we highlight the powerful role of acculturation in African American behavior (physical and mental health). Each study involves a sample of 100 to 300 African Americans. Our purpose is neither to generalize from these samples to all African Americans nor to draw conclusions but rather to begin to explore the role of African American culture in the behavior of African Americans.

To some extent, our point here is to join the many other scholars who emphasize the importance of African American culture to a full understanding of African American behavior and psychology. Unlike those scholars, however, we have the additional goal of destroying and dismantling race, races, and Blacks and Whites once and for all, so that a genuine appreciation of *cultural* diversity someday may be achieved.

Hope Landrine, Ph.D.
Elizabeth A. Klonoff, Ph.D.

Acknowledgments

A brief version of Chapter 3 appeared in Landrine, H., & Klonoff, E. A. (1994). The African-American Acculturation Scale: Development, reliability, validity. *Journal of Black Psychology, 20*(2), 104-127.

The studies of cigarette smoking among African Americans that are reported in Chapter 4 were supported by funds provided by the Cigarette and Tobacco Surtax Fund of the State of California through two of their research programs: the University of California Tobacco-Related Disease Research Program (TRDRP), Grant No. 4RT-0348 to Hope Landrine, and the Department of Health Services Tobacco Control Section program (TCS), Grant No. 92-15385 and Grant No. 94-20962 to Elizabeth A. Klonoff.

We are grateful to Judy Scott and Phyllis Wilkins for their assistance in collecting the data reported in this book.

1

Deconstructing Race and Reviving Culture

A New Approach to "Blacks"[1]

I n recent years, the concept of acculturation has emerged as a promising, nonracist way of explaining and understanding ethnic differences. Acculturation loosely refers to the extent to which ethnic-cultural minorities participate in the cultural traditions, values, beliefs, and practices of their own culture versus those of the dominant "White" society. In the most simple approach to the concept, we can think of acculturation as a continuum from *traditional* to *acculturated* (Table 1.1). Traditional people are those who remain immersed in many of the beliefs, practices, and values of their own culture. In the middle are bicultural people, who have retained the beliefs and practices of their own culture (their culture of origin) but also have assimilated the beliefs and practices of the dominant White society and so participate in two

1

TABLE 1.1 Levels of Acculturation

Traditional	Bicultural	Acculturated
Immersed in culture of origin	Immersed in culture of origin and in dominant culture	Immersed mostly in dominant culture
Usually cannot speak much English	Usually speaks both English (in the world) and native language (at home)	Usually speaks only English and speaks little of or cannot speak native language

very different cultural traditions simultaneously. At the other end of the continuum are highly acculturated people, who have rejected the beliefs and practices of their culture of origin in favor of those of the dominant White society or have never learned their own culture's traditions. Some members of minority groups are highly traditional, some are bicultural, and others are highly acculturated.[2] Still others are *marginal*, and either reject (or never acquired) the beliefs and practices of their own culture or of the dominant culture, as well.

Psychological studies have shown that highly traditional ethnic minorities differ significantly from Whites on a variety of scales and behaviors but that highly acculturated minorities typically do not (e.g., Dana, 1993). Instead, highly acculturated minorities tend to score like Whites on tests and, in many ways, to behave like Whites because, by definition, the beliefs, values, and cognitive styles that characterize highly acculturated minorities are by and large those of the dominant White society's culture. Thus ethnic differences can be understood as a manifestation of an individual's level of acculturation: as a simple reflection of the extent to which ethnic minority people participate—or not—in the beliefs, values, and cognitive styles of the dominant society. Differences between ethnic groups and Whites then do not reflect deficits or deviances on the part of the minority group but instead are reflections of familiarity with and immersion in one culture versus another. The concept of acculturation is refreshing because it provides psychology with a way to conceptualize and explain ethnic differences without resorting to racist, deficit models. By conceptualizing ethnic differences in terms of acculturation, we have the potential to decrease racist understandings of difference and embrace cultural diversity and cultural pluralism. In this sense, the concept of acculturation is the best thing to happen to the study of ethnicity in the history of American psychology.

In addition to providing psychology with a nonracist way to think about difference, the concept of acculturation also provides a rudimentary theory of the relationship between culture and behavior; such a theory is lacking in psychology as a whole, particularly where African Americans are concerned (Jones, 1991b). This is important because a theory of the relationship between culture and behavior allows us to predict and explain the nature and direction of ethnic differences. In the absence of such a theory, ethnic differences that emerge in psychological research are serendipitous. As such, they are difficult to integrate into courses, books, teaching, research, and practice, and they are vulnerable to deficit-model and racist interpretations. The theoretical concept of acculturation makes it possible for us to predict and explain ethnic differences and to understand complex, often inconsistent data within a simple, coherent, nonracist framework.

For example, the concept of acculturation allows us to predict the following, a priori. On any psychological test or behavior, highly acculturated minorities will not differ significantly from Whites whereas, very traditional minorities will, because of specific aspects of the minority person's culture—aspects that the traditional person is immersed in, whereas the acculturated person is not, by definition. Any behavior can be substituted into this general prediction for any ethnic-minority group. For example, we can predict that, in general and irrespective of ethnic minority group, highly acculturated minorities will rely on friends and coworkers for social support and in so doing will not differ from Whites; whereas, very traditional minorities will rely on family and kin for social support and will differ from Whites; and that this difference is due to the familism, filial loyalty and obligation, and distrust of outsiders that characterize many ethnic-minority cultures. The traditional person is immersed in these cultural values and the acculturated one is not, by definition. Being able to predict and explain behavior in this way, so that we can intervene to improve behavior, relationships, and society, is what psychology and social science is about.

MEASURING ACCULTURATION

In light of the importance of acculturation, ways of measuring a person's level of acculturation (acculturation scales) are essential to understanding cultural diversity in human behavior. Thus there are several different acculturation scales for Chinese Americans (Yao, 1979), Japanese Americans (Masuda, Matsumoto, & Meredith, 1970), Cuban Americans (Szapocznik & Kurtines, 1980; Szapocznik, Scopetta, & Kurtines, 1978), Mexican Americans (Cuellar, Harris, & Jasso, 1980; Mendoza, 1989) and some Native American tribes (Hoffman, Dana, & Bolton, 1985). Studies using these scales have found strong relationships between an ethnic minority person's level of acculturation and psychiatric disorders (Burnam, Hough, Karno, Escobar, & Telles, 1987; Montgomery & Orozco, 1985), coronary heart disease (Marmot & Syme, 1976), drug and alcohol abuse (Landrine, Klonoff, & Richardson, 1993; Szapocznik & Kurtines, 1980), cigarette smoking (Landrine, Richardson, Klonoff, & Flay, 1994), hypertension (Dressler, 1982; Dressler, Mata, Chavez, & Viteri, 1987), and many other behaviors and problems.

For example, in a recent study (Landrine, Richardson, et al., 1994), we examined the relationship between Latino acculturation levels and cigarette smoking among more than 4,000 adolescents. We found a strong, linear relationship between smoking and acculturation: Acculturated Latino youth smoked the most, bicultural Latino youth smoked less, and traditional Latinos (those immersed in their own culture) smoked least and usually did not smoke at all. Not only did acculturated Latino youth smoke as frequently as Whites, but multiple regression analyses suggested that they smoked for the same reasons as Whites. We also examined the relationship between acculturation and substance abuse among these Latino youth (Landrine et al., 1993) and found similar results: Traditional Latino youth (immersed in Mexican American culture) did not drink or take drugs but highly acculturated Latino youth did. The children with problematic behavior were not the traditional children, but the acculturated ones.

There are many similar studies of acculturation and behavior, and these are beginning to limit the generalizability of previous research. For example, our study (Landrine, Richardson, et al., 1994) indicated that the well-known finding that Latino youth do not smoke is an inaccurate generalization; traditional Latino youth do not smoke, but acculturated ones do. Again then, the concept of acculturation is important because it not only sheds light on the why of differences between minorities and Whites, but it also highlights and explains differences *within* a minority group. Conceptualizing minority versus majority group differences as a function of cultural beliefs and practices, and conceptualizing the members of a minority group as highly heterogenous with respect to those beliefs and practices, are both integral to a full appreciation and understanding of cultural diversity.

WHAT ABOUT AFRICAN AMERICANS?

The concept of acculturation has been applied to every major ethnic group in the United States except African Americans, and acculturation scales have been developed for every major ethnic group except for African Americans. Why? Why has no one in the discipline applied the concept of acculturation to African Americans? Why has no one developed an African American acculturation scale and conducted studies with it to demonstrate that differences between African Americans and Whites (like the differences between other minorities and Whites) are a simple reflection of the extent to which African Americans are immersed in their own versus the dominant culture? There are two related answers to this question and these reveal the heart of psychology's conceptual paradigm for understanding African Americans versus other ethnic-minority groups. The answers are that (a) psychology as a whole erroneously assumes that African Americans have little or no culture because it was destroyed during slavery (Jones, 1991b), and that (b) psychology conceptualizes African Americans as a race (Jones, 1991b; Yee, Fairchild, Weizmann, & Wyatt, 1993), not as an ethnic or cultural group like other minorities. These two views account for psychology's failure to apply the concept of acculturation—a concept that emphasizes cultural differences—to African Americans.

Psychology's erroneous assumption that African Americans have little or no culture is not shared by the other social sciences. The fact that almost all of the research on African American culture and its African roots comes from those social sciences (history, sociology, and anthropology) is the best evidence for that assertion. This work (e.g., Abrahams, 1970; Crowley, 1977; Genovese, 1974; Guttman, 1974; Hersvokits, 1941; Levine, 1977; Magubane, 1987) is by and large unknown and ignored by psychologists, and thus it is rarely integrated into studies of Black versus White differences, nor is it mentioned in undergraduate or graduate textbooks in psychology. To some extent, this ignorance and neglect of African American culture reflects the narrow, sequestered nature of graduate education in psychology, for that education does not require knowledge of theories or data from the other social sciences. The consequences of the narrowness of graduate education in psychology are serious. Such consequences range from erroneous clinical assumptions and the ensuing misdiagnosis of minorities (Landrine, 1992), to culturally biased and culturally limited models and conclusions in health psychology (Landrine & Klonoff, 1992, 1994), to psychology's peculiar, anachronistic notions about race (Fish, 1995; Yee et al., 1993). Thus psychology's problems with integrating cultural diversity, and with understanding African Americans in particular, could be reduced significantly by broadening graduate education in the field. A few required courses in anthropology, in particular, would significantly improve the discipline's ignorance of culture (Fish, 1995; Landrine & Klonoff, 1992). This change indeed may be a prerequisite if cultural diversity and true pluralism in the discipline's theories and research are to be achieved.

The narrowness of graduate education in psychology probably is not the sole reason that psychology knows so little about African American culture, however. Rather, since its inception, psychology has played a leading role in denying the existence of African American culture; in defining African Americans as a race and nurturing the concept of race; and in attempting to demonstrate that African Americans are intellectually inferior to Whites. The leadership role that psychology has taken in the study of prejudice and racism (e.g., Gordon Allport, James M. Jones, and others), in facilitating desegregation through powerful studies (e.g, Kenneth Clark and Marnie Clark, the early work of Otto Klineberg), and in combating racism (e.g., Phyllis Katz, Bernice Lott and Al Lott, and others) cannot compensate for the racist history and continuing racism of the field. From the racist public statements of G. Stanley Hall (Gould, 1981) to the fraudulent work of Cyril Burt (Kamin, 1974); to Rushton's (1992, 1994) continuation of the craniometric studies[3] that characterized 19th-century science and psychology; to *The Bell Curve* (Herrnstein & Murray, 1994), psychology has been terribly consistent in doing much to denigrate, degrade, and further the disenfranchisement of African Americans. Indeed, the general public's knowledge of psychology's race-IQ studies in particular is undoubtedly a hidden variable in the discipline's difficulty in attracting African Americans. Why would African Americans want to major, let alone pursue graduate education, in a discipline that persists in trying to prove them inferior?

Thus an additional reason that psychology knows little about African American culture is that, on the whole and for the most part, the field has had little interest in it; this is clear in the dearth of psychological research on African American culture and its role in behavior, as well as in the racist models still pursued by too many psychologists.

Psychology's ignorance and neglect of African American culture is but one reason that no one in the discipline has applied the concept of acculturation to African Americans. A second and perhaps more powerful reason is that psychology conceptualizes African Americans as a race rather than as an ethnic group, where race and ethnicity represent two very different paradigms for understanding difference. In this chapter, we argue that African Americans are not a race but are instead an ethnic (cultural) group. Thus, in this book, we argue and demonstrate that acculturation is the best and only appropriate approach to understanding African Americans.[4] Consequently, an exploration of the meaning of race (versus ethnicity) is essential to our purpose and is the focus of the remainder of this chapter.

The major questions to be answered in this chapter are, What is a race and who can be one? How do a people become a race? Why are African Americans regarded as a race? Can a people cease being a race, and if so, can Blacks and Whites cease being races, and become ethnic groups?

ON MAKING (AND UNMAKING) RACES

The term *race* refers to groups that are socially defined (designated) as such on the basis of physical criteria, and *ethnic group* refers to groups that are socially defined on the basis of cultural[5] criteria (Gossett, 1965; Lewotin, Rose, & Kamin, 1984; Littlefield, Liebermann, & Reynolds, 1982; Montagu, 1945, 1962; van den Berghe, 1978). The concept of race tells us to focus on the physical differences between groups and view these as socially important; race tells us to look at how people differ physically and see those physical differences as the explanation for behavioral differences. The concept of ethnicity, on the other hand, tells us to focus on cultural differences between groups and see those as socially important; ethnicity tells us to look at how people differ culturally and to see those cultural differences as the explanation for behavioral variance. The relationship between race and ethnicity is that races are always ethnic groups. That is, groups that have been defined as races always differed culturally from those who defined them as such (van den Berghe, 1978). Consequently, all people with big ears or with brown eyes never have been and are highly unlikely to ever be defined as races because they do not constitute cultures (ethnic groups). Thus, we modify the previous (well-known) definition of race as follows, and provide our own definition of the term:

A race is an ethnic group that has been socially defined as such on the basis of physical criteria.

Several important conclusions follow deductively from this definition of race, and these facilitate a full understanding of precisely what race means.

1. If a race is an ethnic group that simply has been defined as such, then any ethnic group can be defined as a race.
2. If any ethnic group can be defined as a race, then it is necessarily the case that *any* physical criteria (no matter how odd, illogical, or unreliable), can be used to define and delineate races. If any physical criteria can be used to define and delineate races, it is necessarily the case that
   a. The criteria employed to define and delineate (to create) races must vary cross-culturally and (indeed) historically.

If the criteria used to define and delineate races vary from culture to culture then it follows that
   b. An individual's racial classification depends on the local (cultural) criteria for categorizing people into races (on the folk racial taxonomy of the surrounding culture or society).

This means that
   c. An individual can be a member of one race in one culture and of another race in a different culture, such that racial classification thereby is neither stable nor permanent. If any individual can be a member of one race in one culture and of another race in a different culture, then it follows that

3. Races and racial classification cannot possibly have a biological or genetic basis or foundation, unless we believe that one's genes can change from culture to culture. Finally, if ethnic groups are not inherently races but rather are simply defined as such, then it follows that

4. Any ethnic group that has been defined as a race can be undefined as such. Races that have been made can be unmade, races that have been created can be destroyed. Therefore, African Americans and European Americans constitute the Black and White races simply because they have been defined as such, and they need not remain so. African Americans can be undefined as a race and redefined as an ethnic group.

If our definition of race is empirically true (factually correct), then each of the four conclusions above is also necessarily true (according to the principles of logic) because it follows deductively from the definition. Thus, empirical evidence for each of the four conclusions should exist. Some of that evidence is presented below.

Conclusion 1: Any ethnic group can be defined as a race.

Ample evidence for this conclusion comes from history. For example, historical data indicate that many groups now regarded as ethnic groups were once enslaved or exploited by a more powerful ethnic group and were defined as races by that group to justify such treatment. Asians (the Oriental race, Mongoloid race, "yellow man"), Native Americans (the "red man"), Jews, Slavs (who provide the root for the word *slave* because of their long enslavement; Sowell, 1994), and the indigenous Indians of Mexico are but a few examples of ethnic groups who have been enslaved, exploited, or nearly exterminated. All were defined as a race separate from that of their abusers to justify their abuse (Gould, 1981; Sowell, 1994; van den Berghe, 1978).[6] In addition, historical evidence suggests that these groups (as well as the Africans captured in the Atlantic slave trade) were each initially recognized and perceived as ethnic groups (as culturally different), and only later were redefined as races, when religious and other justifications for their vicious, inhumane treatment were less than sufficient (Sowell, 1994). Even in South Africa then, "At first race was not the basis for status differentiation between Europeans and indigenous people. Religion [a cultural difference] was the important criterion. . . . within a generation, however . . . race had supplanted religion" (van den Berghe, 1978, p. 96).

Thus, although American psychology tends to think of African Americans as somehow "inherently" racial, the enslaved Africans were but one of countless ethnic groups who have been defined and treated as races in the world's history of conquest, barbarism, and slavery. Even a cursory perusal of the history of Jews (Greenberg, 1944; Quigley & Glock, 1979; Schaar, 1958), for example, reveals that they were (and in some circles still are) defined, understood, and treated as a race, with all of the allusions that the term *race* entails.

Any ethnic group can be defined as a race, then, and indeed, many have been. Historical data suggest that who has been, is, and (by implication) in the future will be defined as a race is contingent solely upon one ethnic group's desire to exploit, expel, exterminate, or enslave another and on that ethnic group's power to do so—including the power to institutionalize and legitimize racial concepts as justification (supporting ideology) for exploitation/enslavement. Thus, we expand our definition of race to include this historical evidence, as follows:

Races are any ethnic groups that have been socially defined as such on the basis of physical criteria. Races are created from ethnic groups by applying and institutionalizing said criteria if and only if racial constructions are needed to justify the enslavement, exploitation, or expulsion of one ethnic group by another. Races are created only when initial conditions of ethnic-group differences in power exist.

In this sense, race is but a four-letter word, a polite profanity that blames the exploited and enslaved for their exploitation and enslavement.

Conclusion 2: Any physical criteria can be used to delineate races, and such criteria vary cross-culturally.

Historical and anthropological data suggest that a variety of physical and ancestral criteria have been used to categorize people into races, and these criteria vary cross-culturally. The criteria used to define and create races have included everything from the culture of one's parents and grandparents to height, and the ensuing number of races has varied from 2 to 10 or more. For example, the Tutsi in central Africa (a tall group) define themselves as a race separate from and superior to the Twa (a shorter, culturally different group) based on this height difference, and the Tutsi dominate and exploit the Twa (van den Berghe, 1978). The Twa are considered an inferior race just as surely as are African Americans, with all of the trappings and consequences that the concept of *race* entails. Yet, for Tutsi and Twa, race is a question of height.

In Brazil, on the other hand, combinations of hair, eye color, skin color, shape of nose, and thickness of lips are used to define races. Because these physical features can combine in a diversity of ways (e.g., a dark-skinned person can have both thin lips and a narrow nose), Brazilians have a multitude of separate races corresponding to the permutations of these features (Harris, 1964). Alternatively, in Haiti, physical features and ancestry are used to define races in such a complex manner that the 10 children of one Brazilian couple could be categorized by Haitians into 10 different racial groups (Fish, 1995; Harris, 1964).

Thus, although American psychology tends to view race as an immutable, biological category inherent in skin color (or indeed, in a tiny percentage of "Black blood"),[7] this view is empirically incorrect. Race is not inherent in differences in skin color, for many groups defined as separate races are as white-skinned (e.g., Jews) as those from whom they have been differentiated (e.g., Gentiles), and others (e.g., the Twa) are as brown-skinned as those from whom they are defined as separate (e.g., the Tutsi). Instead, any ethnic group can be defined as a race by another ethnic group on the basis of any physical difference (such as height) or ancestral difference, no matter how small, odd, or unreliable the selected differences may be. This is to say that what constitutes a phenotype (physical difference) depends on the phenotypic (physical) features deemed important by a culture; phenotypes are in the eye of the cultural beholder. The number of races created by applying phenotypic criteria is not somehow necessarily two but instead can be any number. The criteria used to define and create races (the taxonomy) vary considerably cross-culturally—and that means that how one is categorized depends on the local taxonomy. The folk racial taxonomy used in the United States is merely one of many.

Consequently, racial classification is not stable but flexible, fluid, and ephemeral. Those who are members of the Black or White race in the United States can be and are classified differently when traveling abroad. As Fish (1995) noted, "individuals can easily change their race by getting on a plane and flying from New York to Salvador [Brazil] or Port-au-Prince [Haiti]. What changes is not their physical appearance but the folk taxonomies by which they are classified" (p. 45).

Thus, the tennis player Yannick Noah once said, "In Africa I am White and in France I am Black" (cited in Fairchild, Yee, Wyatt, & Weizmann, 1995, p. 46). What race is Yannick Noah? The answer is that it depends on where he is. Again, who is Black and who is White is not inherent in appearance or ancestry but is instead decided upon and imposed by a culture. American Blacks and Whites are not inherently, naturally, obviously, or universally different races, any more than are Jews and Gentiles or Tutsi and Twa.

Finally, because the criteria that the United States uses to categorize people into races are merely one set among many, and because those criteria cannot be demonstrated to be better than the very different criteria used by other cultures, America's races cannot be demonstrated to be any more "real" or any less arbitrary than others. America's two races are no more given in nature than Brazil's plethora of races. Black and White are not nature's categories, they are ours.

In light of these anthropological data, we again expand our definition of race as follows:

Races are any ethnic groups that have been socially defined as such on the basis of any arbitrary, culturally relative, and culturally specific physical and/or ancestral criteria. Races are created from ethnic groups by applying and institutionalizing said criteria if and only if racial constructions are needed to justify the enslavement, exploitation, expulsion, or abuse of one ethnic group by another. Races are created only when initial conditions of ethnic-group differences in power exist.

This means that Blacks and Whites constitute different races solely because they were defined as such by European slave traders to justify the Atlantic slave trade and American slavery; the multitude of ethnic groups involved (e.g., Bantu, Zulu, British, Portuguese) were all reduced to a mere two races under conditions in which European slave traders had the power to enslave Africans and to define the various cultures included as constituting a single Black race.

The problem for American psychology, and for Americans more generally, is that we do not experience Blacks and Whites as arbitrary categories. We do not experience ourselves as imposing a racial categorization scheme on people; we do not feel that we are purposefully organizing and interpreting stimuli according to a local taxonomy. Instead, we experience race as something that is passively perceived and indeed received by our senses, against and without our will. Race seems to be something "out there" impinging upon our senses, rather than something in here, ideas in our heads. Because we experience races in this passive manner, we feel in our hearts that they must be real and that to say that they are not is simply silly. Such views are based on erroneous beliefs about the nature of perception.

Some Notes on Human Perception

Perception is rarely a conscious, deliberate, cognitive process. Instead, perception consists of instantaneous, unconscious interpretations and conclusions about stimuli, based on the taxonomies given by one's culture. To perceive is not to passively receive but to automatically, unconsciously impose, interpret, and conclude. Helmholtz (1866/1962) argued this view regarding the perception of objects more than a century ago when he stated that

> the psychological activities that lead us to infer that there in front of us at a certain place there is a certain object of a certain character are generally not conscious activities, but unconscious ones. In their result they are equivalent to a conclusion . . . what seems to differentiate them from a conclusion, in the ordinary sense of the word, is that a conclusion is an act of conscious thought . . . it may be permissible to speak of the psychic acts of ordinary perception as unconscious conclusions, thereby making a distinction between them and so-called conscious conclusions. And while it is true that there has been, and probably always will be, a measure of doubt as to the similarity of the psychic activity in the two cases, there can be no doubt as to the similarity between the results of such unconscious conclusions and those of conscious conclusions. (p. 538)

The view that perception and comprehension are essentially unconscious interpretations and conclusions based upon unconscious, culturally based inferences and categories has been a dominant one in cognitive psychology (e.g., Bransford & McCarrell, 1977; Miller, 1977) and in the psychology of perception (e.g., Gregory, 1970; McArthur & Baron, 1983) for at least the past two decades. According to researchers, for example, we know that a flat gray object stuck to the wall in a classroom is a blackboard with specific functions that are part of being a blackboard. We know all of this not because of the physiological effects of this object on our sensory organs, but instead because of what we bring to the act of perceiving the object. What we bring to the act of perceiving is cultural categories, taxonomies, knowledge, and understandings. We do not *perceive* a blackboard but rather *conclude* a blackboard by "going beyond the information given" to our senses (Bruner's 1957 phrase) to a culture—to a largely unconscious pool of information and categories—that tells us what we are seeing. Thus, we can say a priori that members of a culture that has never seen a blackboard could not possibly categorize the strange object as such, for blackboardness is no more inherent in that object than race is in any particular physical feature.

Perception is an active, culturally driven process through which members of a culture interact with and simultaneously create a world of types of people, actions, groups, and things. It is an active process in the sense that the categories used for carving up the world, as well as the rules for such categorization, are being imposed incessantly upon phenomena. Perception is experienced, however, as the passive receipt of that which is objectively before us because a culture's categories and rules for categorization are the content of the consciousness of its members. Consequently, even using the term *interpretation* for the act of perception, is

> not quite right, because it suggests an imposition upon raw data of a meaning not inherent in them. [In fact, however,] the [cultural] meaning *is prior to the data* which [therefore] will always have the same pre-read [pre-interpreted] shape. [Consequently,] that which appears to be there independently of anything we might say or think about it [is] not independent of [our] verbal and mental categories but is in fact a product of them; and *it is because these categories, rather than being added to perception, are its content* [italics added] that the entities they bring into being seem to be a part of the world in the sense that they were there before there was anyone to perceive them. [What we perceive is] not the result of an interpretive act performed self-consciously on data otherwise available, but the result of an interpretive act performed at so deep a level that it is indistinguishable from consciousness itself. (Fish, 1979, p. 244-245)

In summary, we experience our racial taxonomy as given in nature because our nation's racial categories are the content of our perceptions. Our races seem to be out there, and seem to have been out there before we defined them as such, prior to any act of perception, because we bring our racial taxonomy to the act of perceiving. Our racial taxonomy *is* the perception, and that taxonomy is learned at some point in childhood (precisely when is still being debated by developmental and social psychologists).

That the racial taxonomy is the perception is true for other cultures as well, however—for Brazilians, whose multitude of differently defined races seem as real to them as ours do to us. Our taxonomy nonetheless remains merely one of many, no matter how real the groups it brings into being seem to be. And, because our taxonomy cannot be demonstrated to be superior to any other, our races are as arbitrary as any others. Each of us can and does change races by traveling from culture to culture, with each of the multitude of different races into which we are subsequently categorized understood by the local culture as "obviously" given in our appearance. Which race each of us belongs to depends not on our physical features, but on where (and when) we are, on our context.[8]

Conclusion 3: Race is not a biological or genetic category.

Yannick Noah is of the Black race in one culture and of the White race in another. Unless we believe that his genes change when he flies from France to Africa, we must conclude that race is not a biological or genetic category; it is a social one. Indeed, given that each of us could be classified as a member of a plethora of different races simply by traveling from culture to culture, how could the various races into which we are subsequently categorized possibly differ genetically from each other? The answer is that they could not.

Because racial classification entails an absolutely arbitrary, sociopolitical categorization scheme, groups so defined are necessarily genetically heterogenous. In other words, because phenotypes are in the eye of the cultural beholder and vary from culture to culture, they cannot possibly correspond to genotypes. Thus, it is not surprising that physical anthropologists and geneticists have consistently found that there is significantly greater genetic and biological variance *within* groups socially defined as races than between them (e.g., Lewotin et al., 1984; Littlefield et al., 1982; Polednak, 1989; Vogel & Motulsky, 1986). In statistical language, this is to say that the genetic variance within socially defined racial groups far exceeds the variance between them, such that races do not differ significantly genetically.

Our point here is not to deny the enormous genetic variance in the human population, for such variability (e.g., in HLA antigens; in specific heritable diseases, etc., see Polednak, 1989) has been found quite consistently. Rather, our point is that (a) the many human populations who differ genetically from each other have been lumped together in the arbitrary social category White; (b) others who differ from each other by genetic criteria have been lumped together into the arbitrary social category Black; and (c) others who share major genetic characteristics (e.g., the HbS gene responsible for sickle cell anemia) have been arbitrarily categorized as being White (Mediterranean populations), Black (Africans and African Americans), and Asian (Far Eastern populations, including India). Such data indicate clearly that racial categories do not mirror genetic populations and are not based on genetic criteria. Certainly, several genetic populations exist, but these do not mirror America's races any more than they mirror Haiti's races or Brazil's races. This is why the idea that racial differences in scores on IQ tests are the result of genetic differences between arbitrarily defined races is ludicrous on its face and is rejected as such by the American Anthropological Association.[9] The arbitrary and social nature of racial taxonomies, as well as the ephemeral, culturally variable criteria for membership in a race, form the basis of anthropology's conclusion that racial taxonomies are scientifically meaningless. By *scientifically meaningless* anthropologists mean that races cannot be demonstrated to exist out there in nature as obvious, natural, universal, stable, or genetic populations.

Because races are scientifically meaningless does not mean that they are socially or politically meaningless, however. Rather, because race is a social and political category, it has enormous social and political correlates and consequences. As we demonstrated earlier, races are created under a specific set of initial social and political conditions in order to explain and justify those conditions; when race is imposed on ethnic groups and races are thereby created, it is clear that race is a sociopolitical category. We now further suggest that race is then subsequently argued to be a scientific category in order to increase its legitimacy and to deny the contemporary relevance of the initial conditions under which races were created. Specifically, by arguing that race is a scientific category, psychology increases the legitimacy, the respectability, of the concept of race. The ontological status of races is raised from that of arbitrary, politically motivated creations to that of facts of nature. Misrepresenting this social and political category as a scientific one thereby exempts the concept of race from social and political criticism—from being the subject of social protest—and renders it vulnerable only to scientific criticism. Consequently, radical and conservative civil rights groups alike never have challenged the idea that African Americans are a race but rather have focused on the mistreatment of that (ostensible) race. When elevated to the status of a scientific concept, only scientists—not ordinary parents—can challenge race at its most fundamental and socially significant level. Given how slowly science proceeds, disguising race as a scientific category assures that race and races will persist.

In addition, to argue that race is a scientific category denies the relevance of the initial conditions under which races were created. If the races that we recognize in our taxonomy exist out there in nature, then they necessarily existed prior to slavery and necessarily exist after slavery. Slavery then is irrelevant to race in America; the racial status of African Americans and of Whites does and would exist with or without slavery. Slavery is then rendered a lamentable, historical event of little contemporary consequence, a view that many Americans no doubt hold. By disguising races as scientific statuses, we forget that *without slavery there would be no races*, there would be no such things as Blacks and Whites. Presenting socially defined races as if they had scientific status thus not only legitimizes race but also facilitates the historical amnesia necessary for maintaining the concept of race. Only by removing that cloak of scientific legitimacy can we remember that races are not born but made. If they were made, then they can be unmade. In other words, if ethnic groups can be defined as and transformed into races (i.e., racialized) in order to explain and justify their initial expulsion, enslavement, or exploitation, then it follows deductively that when the initial enslavement or exploitation has ended, the stage is set for ethnic groups to be undefined as races.[10] We can now return to our major argument.

Conclusion 4: If races can be created, then they can be destroyed.

As demonstrated earlier, a diversity of ethnic groups throughout history have been racialized (defined as races), yet many of those groups are no longer regarded as races. This means that ethnic groups that have been racialized can be deracialized (undefined as races) and reethnicized (redefined as ethnic groups). For example, Americans and American psychology now understand Jews, Italians, and Irish as ethnic groups; yet, earlier in history, we regarded them as separate races (Gailey, 1994). These groups are then *former races*, and they are not the only ones. Native Americans are another, important example of a former race.

In the past, European Americans defined Native Americans as a race to be exterminated. Now, however, Native Americans are deracialized and reethnicized; racial distinctions have been replaced by ethnic ones. After hundreds of years of thinking about and treating Native Americans as the inferior, uncivilized, backward "red man" race to be exterminated, who in America or American psychology thinks of Native Americans as a race anymore? Who in psychology conducts studies to argue that Native Americans are intellectually inferior to Whites? Who in psychology is arguing that the enormous poverty suffered by many Native Americans stems from their innate, intellectual inferiority? No one, no one at all; instead, we associate these kinds of research projects and arguments with African Americans alone. Yet, many years ago, when this nation regarded Native Americans as a race, research on them took precisely this form, namely, studies designed to demonstrate their inferiority (Gould, 1981), studies that lent legitimacy to Native Americans' racialized status.[11] Native Americans are perhaps the best historical example of *American race making* and of the deracializing and reethnicizing of an American ethnic group.[12]

One consequence of the fact that races created can also be destroyed is that many people in the United States are members of former races. Many Americans can say, "Yes, I used to be a member of a race, but I'm not anymore," or, "Yeah, we were once a race, but now we're just an ethnic group." Being able to make such (empirically accurate) statements is evidence that race varies not only cross-culturally but historically as well. African Americans appear to be the only exception to this historical pattern; they remain the only racialized American ethnic group. African Americans are the last vestige of centuries of American race making.

A discussion of the reasons that African Americans remain the only racialized, American (minority) ethnic group is beyond the scope and purpose of this chapter. We can hypothesize, however, that the racialized status of African Americans (initially necessary to justify slavery) probably persists to justify that past— to justify the history of slavery in America. This is because slavery was a bitter, bloody, moral, and political issue and source of national embarrassment and conflict when it began and throughout its long history (Myrdal, 1944; Sowell, 1978a). The nation may need to continue to think of African Americans and European Americans as separate races to be reconciled with that history. The question, however, is not why African Americans remain racialized but if they must remain so. Consistent with the evidence presented here, our answer is no, and that indeed is the point of this chapter and of this book. African Americans and European Americans need not remain conceptualized as racial groups. Instead, African Americans can (and we believe should) be reethnicized, regarded as an ethnic group whose culture is understood as the genesis and explanation for the ways in which they differ from European Americans, as well as from each other (levels of acculturation). In addition, the fact that Native Americans have been deracialized and reethnicized suggests that African Americans can be as well. This is because the historical and contemporary treatment and status of Native Americans most closely parallels that of African Americans. There are several, important advantages to redefining African Americans and European Americans as ethnic groups (to deracializing Blacks and Whites) and to rejecting the concept of race in the process.

FIVE REASONS TO
UNMAKE AMERICA'S RACES

1. *Race is more than a word; rather, it is also a theoretical model of difference.* The theoretical model of difference entailed in the concept of race is harmful to individuals, groups, and society; is morally repugnant; lacks empirical evidence and thereby does not advance science; and maintains racial stratification.

2. *The concept of race racializes European Americans as well as African Americans.* Race thereby obstructs psychology's understanding of Whites because it ignores cultural differences among the diversity of cultures defined as the White race. To reject the concept of race entails rejecting the concept of a White race and bringing the various cultures of Whites into the foreground where they can facilitate psychology's ability to understand behavior.

3. *The concept of race is unscientific.* Psychology's continuing use of it (despite its rejection by other sciences) renders the discipline ludicrous in the eyes of other sciences, as well as in the eyes of much of the public. Consequently, psychology as science and practice is not advanced by the concept, and neither science nor society is served.

4. *As long as the concept of race remains, neither tolerant cultural pluralism in society nor an appreciation of diversity in psychology can be achieved,* for these are negated by maintaining a superior, White race.

5. *As long as the concept of race remains in psychology and (thus) in the public consciousness, powerful persons and groups remain free to use it.* Any of the many, growing ethnic groups (e.g., Latinos) in this country can be defined as races, and will be so defined under specific social and economic conditions. Psychology must reject the concept of race if only to prevent this, because psychology alone maintains the concept. The only way to do so is to deracialize African Americans (and with them, European Americans). Each of these points is addressed below.

The theoretical model of difference entailed in race is unacceptable. To conceptualize an ethnic group as a race, and to conceptualize that same ethnic group as an ethnic group, are two very different approaches with vast implications. This is because race and ethnicity are more than simple words, they are theoretical models of and basic assumptions about the nature of difference. To conceptualize an ethnic group as a race is to begin with the assumption that its members differ genetically and permanently from other ethnic groups, and it is to endorse the theoretical model that their behavioral differences are a function of these immutable differences. This is what Americans mean by race and understand a race to be, even though such views are inconsistent with empirical evidence. Consequently, race is an invidious and provocative way of conceptualizing ethnic groups: Race creates, it brings into being, types of people, people who belong to one versus another permanent category into which they are born and from which they cannot exit. It brings into being a world that fundamentally is and always will be divided and closed. Racial classification simultaneously carries a stigma that ethnic classification does not. This is because the *purpose* of racial classification is to render some ethnic groups inherently honorable and superior and others innately degraded and inferior (Epperson, 1994; Gran, 1994). That this is the purpose of racial classification is supported by historical data on the conditions under which races are created. Indeed, all of us know that in the commonsense understanding of the term, *race* not only means genetically different types of people, but it also entails the assumption that some groups are superior to others. In the final analysis, this is precisely why the term arouses passions.

To classify ethnic groups as races, then, is not to simply or merely call attention to difference. Rather, it is to create permanent, genetically different types of people, some of whom are innately superior to and inherently more worthy and valuable than others. When we conceptualize an ethnic group as a race, then (no matter which ethnic-group-cum-race we have in mind) we mean these things, and this is how that group is understood (and treated) in science and society. Such concepts do not enhance our scientific understanding (for such views are inconsistent with scientific evidence); do not serve society (but rather, encourage antagonism among ethnic groups); harm the ethnic group defined as the inferior race; reduce research to efforts to legitimate races; reinforce racial stratification; and are morally repugnant. This is what it meant for Native Americans to be a race; this is how this nation once understood and treated them.

Conceptualizing ethnic groups as ethnic groups, however, is quite a different matter. To conceptualize an ethnic group as an ethnic group is to begin with the assumption that they differ historically and culturally from other ethnic groups, and it is to endorse the theoretical model that their behavioral differences are a function of these historical and cultural differences. This is what Americans mean by ethnicity in their shared, common-sense understandings of the term, and it is why the concept does not raise passions. Consequently, ethnicity is a nonprovocative way of conceptualizing ethnic groups: Ethnicity creates, it brings into being, types of cultures and histories rather than types of people. It creates a world of people who participate, temporarily or permanently but always by choice, in one set of traditions, values, and practices versus another. The categories created are neither permanent nor stigmatized, and people cross ethnic lines (cultural lines) whenever they choose. Ethnicity thereby brings into being a world that fundamentally is and always will be complex, pluralistic, and open.

Our understanding of ethnic groups as open and fluid, and of ethnic boundaries as permeable (unlike our notion of race) is consistent with anthropological and sociological data. Those data indicate that ethnic group identity and membership are so fluid that people can and do change ethnic groups whenever they like. They do so by engaging in rituals for membership in another group; by adopting the religious, dietary, and other practices of the culture, and/or by simply calling themselves members of an alternative ethnic group (for examples, see Cohen, 1969; Enloe, 1980; Nagel, 1982; Nagel & Olzak, 1982; Neilsen, 1986; Novak, 1972; Olzak, 1982; Portes, 1984). Thus the concept of ethnicity does enhance our scientific understanding (for such views are consistent with scientific evidence); does *not* harm ethnic groups defined as ethnic groups; encourages research on cultural diversity, and encourages intercultural appreciation and exchange. This is what it means for Native Americans to be an ethnic group; this is how the nation now regards them.

The differences between thinking of Native Americans as a race and thinking of them as an ethnic group are significant and extend far beyond changes in the content of psychological research on them. For example, when we understood Native Americans as an inferior race, no one wanted to be one. Now that we understand Native Americans as an ethnic group, however, just about everybody wants to be Native American (Deloria, 1983). How many times have we each heard people claim that there are Native Americans in their ancestral line; that there is a "princess" of some particular tribe in their family tree; that they are thereby one eighth or one sixteenth Native American? These claims are so common that the Native American scholar Vine Deloria, Jr. (1983) called them the "Indian-grandmother complex."[13] Although such claims are problematic because they represent what Rosaldo called "imperialist nostalgia,"[14] they nonetheless reveal the difference between race and ethnicity: Everyone wants to be Native American, but no one wants to be Black, although both groups are similarly poor and disadvantaged historically and currently. The reason is that the ethnic category is inherently neutral (and fantasized to be positive), whereas the racial category is inherently negative.

In summary, the theoretical model of difference entailed in the concept of race is repugnant, unscientific, and socially divisive. The model of difference entailed in the concept of ethnicity, on the other hand, is consistent with scientific evidence and does not encourage discrimination against or conflict among ethnic groups. Society's treatment and evaluation of African Americans, and psychology's research on African Americans, would both change simply by deracializing and reethnicizing African Americans. The truth of this assertion is seen in the history of Native Americans. This is not to naively suggest, however, that racial stratification and racism will end by reethnicizing African Americans, for these certainly will not simply disappear (Harrison, 1994), any more than they disappeared for Native Americans. It is to suggest that the social evaluation and treatment of an ethnic group in our society is significantly improved by what psychology calls that group. Given that there is no scientific justification for calling African Americans a race, the increase in their social evaluation and treatment that would follow from calling them an ethnic group is more than adequate justification to do so. Indeed, the harm caused to African Americans by the concept of race (which psychology alone maintains) was one of the major reasons that Yee et al. (1993) argued that psychology's use of the concept of race violates the ethical principles of the American Psychological Association.

Race dismisses the cultures of Whites and thereby obstructs the progress of psychology as a science. The concept of race entails grievous consequences, not only for those lumped together as Black, but also for those lumped together as White. A multitude of genetically and culturally different groups have been classified as simply being White. Doing so ignores, derides, and dismisses the cultures entailed and obstructs psychology's ability to understand human behavior. For example, studies have demonstrated significant and important cultural and subsequent behavioral differences among Polish (Kantowitz, 1992), Italian (Quadagno, 1981), Irish (Clark, 1992), Greek (Kourvetaris, 1981), and Jewish Americans (Farber, Mindel, & Lazerwitz, 1981; Shapiro, 1992). As we have argued elsewhere (Landrine & Klonoff, 1992; Landrine, Klonoff, & Brown-Collins, 1992), such cultural differences may well account for the unexplained (error) variance within White samples. Italian Americans, for example, have some beliefs about the nature and causes of illness that differ from those of other ethnic groups, and these cultural differences lead them to respond in a way that differs from other Whites where health-related issues are concerned (e.g., Moss & Cappannari, 1960). Consequently, knowing about Italian American culture is relevant to appropriate treatment interventions, as Taylor (1991, p. 266) demonstrated clearly with a case example.

How much of the variance in White samples can be attributed to differences among the diversity of ethnic groups involved? To what extent would data in social, clinical, health, developmental, and feminist psychology be different, had researchers assessed the cultural background of the White subjects? The various principles established in many areas of psychology, based on studies of White samples, are problematic in the sense that we do not know if they hold for African Americans or for other ethnic minority groups. The question, however, is whether such principles even hold for various White ethnic groups. Would findings based on Whites hold for samples that are entirely or predominantly Jewish or Indian (from India—who are classified as White despite their phenotypic differences)? Are results found with White samples simply a function of the predominant ethnic group that participated? Would a study based on an Amish sample generalize to other Whites? To whom, exactly, then, do data from psychological experiments apply? For whom are psychology's principles the case? These questions are serious ones about the nature and meaning of psychological knowledge in light of the discipline's tendency to ignore (not only ethnic minorities, but also) the cultures of White research participants.

The answer to these questions is that psychology does not know to whom its data and principles apply.

Thus, obscuring the differences (e.g., in history, family structure, and religious, health, child rearing, and dietary practices) among European American ethnic groups by categorizing them together as the White race cannot possibly be said to serve the goals of a science of behavior. To imply through the use of the term *Whites* that American Greeks and Jews and Armenians and Italians and Finns are "the same" behaviorally, socially, or even genetically is to make not a scientific but a political statement. The truth of that assertion is clear in the fact that these particular White groups have been demonstrated to differ from each other not only culturally, but also in specific genetic characteristics. For example, many Ashkenazic Jews have the gene for Tay-Sachs disease, and this gene does not appear in Sephardic Jews, let alone in other Whites. Many Greeks and Italians have a gene for sickle cell anemia and sickle cell trait (HbS, HbAS, HbSS), and these genes do not appear in other Whites (except Sephardic Jews) but instead appear in those classified as Black and as "Asian." Many Armenians have a gene for Familial Mediterranean Fever, and this gene does not appear in other Whites. And, many Finns have a gene for Von Willebrand disease, as well as a gene for Aspartylglucosaminuria, and these genes do not appear in other Whites (Polednak, 1989). The reason that psychology regards these European American ethnic groups as members of the White race therefore is not because of any phenotypic or even genotypic similarity. Regarding them as a race clearly is based not on scientific but on political criteria, and psychology's insistence on doing so serves, supports, and advances not science but racism. The concept of a White race obscures the historical, cultural, political, and genetic differences among European American ethnic groups as surely as the concept of a Black race obscures the differences among the three distinct cultural and genetic groups lumped together as American Blacks (see Sowell, 1978b, on the diversity among Blacks).

In summary, the concept of race has racialized European Americans and rendered psychology's knowledge applicable to White people in general, but to no White ethnic group in particular. Psychology's ability to highlight the variables that predict and control human action has not been advanced by the concept of a White race any more than it has been advanced by the concept of a Black race.

The irony is that psychology's claim that race is a scientific category based on genetic criteria is undermined most by regarding phenotypically and genotypically diverse European Americans as the White race. Facilitating a full understanding of White behavior by increasing the variance explained by culture and ethnicity is a second reason to deracialize Blacks and Whites and to reject the concept of race.

Race is not a scientific category. A third reason to deracialize African Americans and reject the concept of race is that race is not a scientific concept or category. As noted earlier here, scientists from a diversity of disciplines (anthropology, biology, genetics) have all rejected race as a scientifically valid category and understand it as the social and political construct it always has been. How can psychology insist that it is right about race and that all other sciences are wrong? How can psychology maintain a concept that has been rejected on empirical grounds by the vast majority of other sciences, yet simultaneously insist that it, too, is a science?[15] To persist in employing such a construct is to dismiss the work of colleagues in other disciplines, and by so doing, to diminish the stature of psychology in the eyes of those sciences and of the world. How many scientists (and their families and friends) fail to seek treatment or advice from psychologists because our widely publicized use of the concept of race leads them to regard us as uninformed at best? How many citizens regard psychology as a simplistic, racist pseudoscience to be dismissed and ignored because of psychology's well-known views about race? How many minorities refuse to major in psychology

and avoid seeking help from psychologists because they are aware
of the discipline's views on race and are offended by those? What
do anthropologists, who have published statements against psychology's claims about race (see note 8), think of psychology?
What does the United Nations Educational, Scientific, and Cultural Organization (UNESCO) think of psychology, given that
they have repeatedly published statements similar to those of
anthropologists (see Yee et al., 1993)?

The answers to these questions are obvious. They are the basis
for our view that psychology's retention of a concept widely
regarded as unscientific obstructs the advancement of psychology
as a science and practice and does not serve, but instead harms,
the public and society.

*Cultural pluralism and diversity are obstructed by the concept of
a "White" race.* As this nation moves toward the 21st century,
the percentage of ethnic minorities continues to increase. Some
have projected that in the next 20 to 25 years, America's ethnic
minorities will constitute the majority of the population, and
Whites (European American ethnic groups) will be a numerical
minority (U.S. Bureau of the Census, 1989). This means that, if
our country is to survive, then all Americans must learn a great
deal about the cultures of the variety of ethnic groups who
constitute Americans, and we must create and learn ways to
understand ethnic differences that build bridges among ethnic
communities.

We suggest that this kind of tolerant, cultural pluralism cannot be achieved so long as the concept of race remains attached
to European Americans. To retain the concept means that European American ethnic groups will continue to be regarded as
constituting a permanent, genetically different, innately superior
White race, whereas everyone else merely belongs to specific
ethnic groups. How can we learn to tolerate, let alone appreciate,
the cultural differences among the nation's many old, new, and
future ethnic groups, while simultaneously regarding European
American cultural groups as a united, superior White race? How

can we embrace cultural diversity while denying the importance, and indeed, the existence of the European American cultures of Whites? We cannot.

Thus, so long as European Americans remain a race, culture is neither elevated nor appreciated, but rather dismissed and derided as a fetish relevant only to minorities and "exotic" people. In this context, discussions of diversity are necessarily racist because they inevitably entail analyses of how "those minorities" differ from a tacit, superior, monolithic, White-race norm. In the context of a White race, discussions of diversity merely discover "primitives" and "natives" whose cultural differences reproduce and support the social hierarchies purportedly challenged by the focus on diversity. In the context of a White race, discussions of diversity necessarily maintain ethnic stratification and antagonism. One of the most important reasons to deracialize Whites and Blacks and to reject the concept of race, then, is the nation's need to establish and maintain peaceful, tolerant, and cooperative relations among ethnic groups, a need that is more pressing now than it has ever been in our nation's history.

Immigration and its discontents: On the future of race making. The current wave of immigration, and the complex issues it has elicited, are nothing new in this nation. Rather, contemporary debates about pluralism and multiculturalism are identical to those that have arisen in the past (since the 1700s) in response to immigration (Postiglione, 1983). Indeed, the contemporary form of these debates began in the 1920s, in response to the 33 million immigrants who had arrived in the country during the prior 100 years. In the 1920s, and in the present, immigration led Whites to fear for their jobs and their economic security. In addition, and more important, immigration also led Whites to fear that they would lose their way of life. Consequently, the White response to immigration always has been to ask what is an American or what does it mean to be an American (Lambert & Taylor, 1990; Postiglione, 1983). Debates about multiculturalism and attempts to curtail immigration always have been part of the answer to that question. Thus, in the 1920s and in the present, we debate what kind of history should be taught in schools, attempt to pass legislation making English the official language of the land, and argue that illegal immigration is the major problem the nation faces. Whether these debates occur in the 1920s in response to Jewish and non-Jewish immigrants from southern and eastern Europe, or in the 1990s in response to immigrants from Haiti, Cuba, Mexico, and Southeast Asia, the debate is fundamentally about who and what an American is. This debate is acted out in arguments regarding what notion or concept of Americans will be supported by national policy and by public funds. To fund bilingual education is to say that Americans are bilingual; to fund health and educational programs for destitute immigrants is to say something about who and what an acceptable American is. These policy issues raised passions in the 1920s and raise them in the 1990s, not because of the federal deficit, but because they go to the heart of a nation's identity.

In the past, the debate about diversity—about who and what an American is—always came to the same conclusion, namely, that a prototypical American is a white-skinned person of northern European descent; those who do not meet that description at least should strive to do so. Perhaps this conclusion could be reached because White Americans of northern European descent were the numerical majority, with the power and privilege to make the common culture in their own image and to legitimize their art, language, and foods as the cultural standard against which all others were judged inferior. In the present, however, salsa has replaced ketchup as the American condiment, and ethnic groups (African Americans included) have little desire to relinquish their cultures and become White (Lambert & Taylor, 1990). Likewise, in the present and for the first time in American history, immigration means that White Americans will be the minority group of the future; in some states (Hawaii, California), that already is the case. In the present, it is clear that immigration means that Whites will lose their privileged status as the numerical majority group, and thereby as the group that defines the nation's common culture and cultural values. Thus, there is reason to suspect that in the future, the debates may need to take another, more radical form, if those debates are not to come again to the conclusion that Americans are White, thereby maintaining the social order as we always have known it.

One form the debate can take is a racial one. Because the concept of race remains, and because any ethnic group can be racialized, one radical, extreme way that powerful Whites can resolve contemporary issues is to define any of the new or future ethnic groups as a separate race. To do so is easy, and indeed, history suggests that making races is perhaps one of the easiest things for a nation to accomplish. Subsequent pseudoscientific justification (from psychology) for racializing the ethnic group can and will be found, as it always has been found in the past, whether for Jews, Native Americans, Italians, Irish, or African Americans. Everything from economic depressions to rising crime rates and the dissolution of the American family can be blamed on the new race, as has happened in the past. Fears regarding what an American is and regarding the privileged, majority status of Whites can then be resolved by forcibly deporting the alien race and revising U.S. immigration policies accordingly. Before regarding this scenario as alarmist, we suggest that one merely consider American and world history to understand just how ordinary this scenario is. For example, in his controversial book, *Alien Nation*, Peter Brimelow (1995) noted that the United States would consist primarily of people of color by the year 2050 and asked what being an American could mean in such a context. Brimelow suggests that immigration laws be changed to restrict immigration of people of color and encourage immigration of White Europeans, so that Whites could retain their numerical majority and capacity to define the common culture.

Thus a final important reason to deracialize Blacks and, in particular, Whites and reject the concept of race is that, so long as the concept of race remains, the United States is free to use it as it has in the past, for the same reasons. Psychology must dismantle race if only to prevent future race making.

SUMMARY

We have established that African Americans and European Americans are Black and White races simply because they have been designated as such. We have demonstrated that racial classification is political rather than scientific and that racial categories are arbitrary, flexible, and ephemeral. We have further demonstrated that groups defined as races can be undefined as such and reethnicized. We have presented five compelling reasons to deracialize Whites and Blacks, and we believe that it is of the utmost importance that American psychology do so, so that the nation can do so. In Appendix A, we outline the steps that psychology can take to rid itself of race, and we demonstrate that the stage has been set for such change.[16]

Given that African Americans are not inherently a race but are instead inherently an ethnic group, the most appropriate approach to the study of their behavior is to examine their culture, their varying degrees of immersion in it (levels of acculturation), and the role that this plays in their behavior. In this book, we do precisely that. In many important ways, other scholars in African American psychology have moved away from studies of African Americans as a race and toward studies of African American culture and its African roots as the lathe of African American behavior (e.g., Asante, 1988; Baldwin, 1981). Recent theoretical and empirical work in African American psychology not only stresses the importance of African American culture in African American behavior (e.g., Jones, 1991a), but also highlights the benefits of remaining immersed in the values, assumptions, and styles of that culture (e.g., Kambon, 1992; Myers, 1988). Books and articles on this Afrocentric worldview and on a culturally saturated, African-centered psychology abound (e.g., Nobles, 1986), and these efforts are consistent with ours.

Thus this book focuses on our work to develop an African American Acculturation Scale (AAAS), on our theoretical model of African American acculturation, and on the preliminary studies that we have conducted, using the AAAS as a tool for understanding African American behavior. This research is consistent with the many recent efforts to bring African American culture to the foreground of the study of African American behavior and to, in effect, reject race and reethnicize African Americans. Our work differs from that growing body of literature only in the sense that we have adopted language and constructs (e.g., acculturation) from the more general study of ethnic groups. We believe that the advantage of doing so, of thinking about African Americans in terms of levels of acculturation, is that we render the study of African American behavior consistent with the study of the behavior of other American ethnic groups. In the final analysis, however, we are saying what Nobles (1986), Asante (1988), Baldwin (1981), and others have said: that African Americans must be understood in terms of their culture; that differences between African Americans and other ethnic groups are cultural; and that differences among African Americans similarly reflect varying degrees of immersion in the culture. Thus, the plethora of concepts (e.g., African self-consciousness, racial-identity, and the like) currently used to explain African American behavior are all fully consistent with our concept of African American acculturation. These concepts and their associated scales represent and assess aspects or dimensions of African American culture; studies that have employed these concepts and scales have demonstrated that degrees of immersion in these aspects of the culture predict and explain behavior. These concepts and scales, and the findings that have resulted from using them, can all be subsumed under and rendered coherent by reconceptualizing them in terms of African American acculturation.

NOTES

1. A basic contention of this book is that there is no scientific or other rational substance to the so-called races customarily identified with the labels "Black" and "White." However, for typographical reasons, we will not emphasize the hollowness of these terms with quotation marks on every usage.

2. There are a variety of complex, theoretical models of acculturation and of biculturalism, but here we allude only to the simplest model. For discussions of these models, see LaFromboise, Coleman, and Gerton, 1993; Martinez and Mendoza, 1984; Padilla, 1980; and Szapocznik et al., 1978. These models will not be discussed in this book. Our purpose here is not to discuss or adopt specific models of acculturation and biculturalism, but rather, to begin to apply the most rudimentary concept of acculturation to African Americans.

3. Craniometry refers to studies in which the size of skulls or the weight of the brains of ethnic groups and the sexes were measured (see Gould, 1981) and compared, with the hope that men and Whites would have bigger brains than minorities and women. If desired differences in brain weight or skull size were found, these data were then used to argue that ethnic minorities and women were innately intellectually inferior to Whites and men, despite the lack of data demonstrating that bigger brains mean higher intelligence. Such studies characterized and captivated the attention of 19th-century psychology, science, and the public, and they were regularly published in the newspapers of the 1800s. Like race-IQ studies, these studies led to further discrimination and racism against African Americans and Native Americans. The majority of craniometric studies, however, did not find the hoped-for results. Rather, minorities and women had brains as big as or bigger than those of Whites and men, and the brains of the poor were typically larger than those of the wealthy.

Gould (1981), who presents the history of craniometry in detail, argued that craniometry died in part because its data failed to support racist and sexist ideology. Craniometry was replaced by psychometry (the use of IQ and other mental tests), and a measure on which minorities did not fare as well as Whites was finally found. The historical connection between craniometry and psychometry is a direct one, in that everyone from Binet to Maria Montessori conducted such studies. Rushton (1992, 1994) has resurrected craniometric studies of African Americans and women. He is not alone: Jensen and Johnson (1994) often cite extremely small correlations between IQ scores and skull size as their proof for the heritability of scores on IQ tests. Given that neither scores on IQ tests nor brain size has been demonstrated to measure intelligence, the proof is questionable at best.

Craniometry left a mark on America in the form of the unconscious belief that a big brain means higher intelligence. The legacy of craniometry is clear in the American tendency to call those we consider unintelligent "pin-heads" or "peabrains." It also is no doubt the basis for the country's tendency to present superintelligent, superior alien beings as having huge heads; indeed, the fictional film character E.T. had an enlarged head. It is hard enough to rid our souls of the legacy of the 19th-century pseudoscience of craniometry without Rushton reviving it on the eve of the 21st century. Perhaps phrenology (the pseudoscience of measuring personality by feeling the bumps on the skull) will be revived as well.

4. Racism, of course, is an equally important factor to study when attempting to understand African Americans, and, thus, by focusing on acculturation, we do not wish to imply that racism should be ignored. We believe that racism and acculturation are both important. In later chapters here, our own research on

racism, using our new scale, *The Schedule of Racist Events*, is reported and integrated with our work on acculturation.

    5. A culture can be defined as a highly specific pool of information, categories, rules for categorization, intersubjective meanings, collective representations, and ways of knowing, understanding, and interpreting stimuli, as a result of a common history (Landrine et al., 1992; Shore, 1991; Shweder & LeVine, 1984). To be a member of a culture is to share its taxonomies, categorization schemes, knowledge, and ways of perceiving and understanding self and others. Culture operates largely at the unconscious level, like an unwritten dictionary that tells its members what things are and what they mean—how to process, evaluate, and interpret the world (Landrine, 1992). Culture is more of a cognitive and perceptual than a behavioral variable (Shore, 1991). It would be beneficial for readers to bear this definition in mind throughout this chapter.

    Many anthropologists and ethnoscientists define culture as knowledge or information (e.g., Basso & Selby, 1976; D'Andrade, 1981; Geoghegan, 1971; Shweder & LeVine, 1984) and estimate this pool of information to consist of several million "chunks" (D'Andrade, 1981). Our definition is consistent with these in emphasizing the cognitive rather than the behavioral (religious and child-rearing practices, arts, music) aspects of culture. This is because, to be a member of a culture is less a question of what one does and more a matter of how and what one perceives, believes, and understands—which then predict what one does.

    6. This is not meant to suggest that slavery requires racial ideology, for in some cases (e.g., ancient Greece and Rome), it existed without defining slaves as a separate race. Enslaved/exploited populations are only defined as a separate race when such definitions are necessary to justify the group's abuse. Such was the case in Mexico, Brazil, the United States (with respect to Native Americans, Asians, and Africans), Nazi Germany, and countless other nations. For a general treatment of the topic, see Sowell (1994). See Westermann (1955) on ancient Greek and Roman slavery; Hellie (1982) and Lewis (1990) for accounts of other slavery systems, and van den Berghe (1978) on the construction of races in Mexican, Brazilian, U.S., and South African slavery and racial stratification systems.

    7. Membership in the Black race is not defined by phenotypic (physical) features but by ancestry; individuals who appear White (e.g., blond hair, blue eyes) are categorized as Black if they can be demonstrated to have any African ancestry (Davis, 1991). This one-drop (of Black blood) rule was initiated at the end of slavery to prevent mulatto former slaves from claiming to be White, and it persists today. For an insightful presentation of the history of the legal definition of Black in the United States, see Davis, 1991.

    8. Because categorization schemes are culturally and historically relative (viz., based on context), race is far from the only basic category that is fluid, flexible, and ephemeral. For example, precisely what constitutes a child or an adolescent has not been stable historically or cross-culturally (Aries, 1962; Benedict, 1950; Kett, 1976). Indeed, even within the United States, the taxonomy for people of different ages has changed considerably. There was a point in American history where children and adolescents, as we know them, did not exist. These two ostensibly "natural," real groups were understood as smaller adults and as such, they worked for a living. The idea that children and adolescents were groups

separate from adults (differing biologically and thereby behaviorally from them) and requiring protection and education evolved primarily in response to the Industrial Revolution (see Aries, 1962; Friendberg, 1965; Gillis, 1981; Kessen, 1979). American children and adolescents are relatively recent cultural inventions, and their creation has been much like the creation of races. Thus, taxonomies for categorizing people into basic groups such as children versus adults, or Blacks versus Whites, have been and remain contingent upon culture and era.

9. The American Anthropological Association (AAA) has adopted several resolutions rejecting research that draws racist conclusions, rejecting the concept of race, and rejecting the idea that "racial" differences in scores on IQ tests are genetic. Such resolutions were adopted in 1961, 1969, 1971, 1972, and again in 1995. The 1995 resolution was published in the January 1995, issue of the *Anthropology Newsletter* and was in response to the book *The Bell Curve* (Herrnstein & Murray, 1994) which was attacked by anthropologists in that same issue. In the new AAA Resolution on Race and Intelligence, anthropologists stated,

> The American Anthropological Association is deeply concerned by recent public discussions which imply that intelligence is biologically determined by race. Repeatedly challenged by scientists, nevertheless these ideas continue to be advanced. Such discussions distract public and scholarly attention from and diminish support for the collective challenge to ensure equal opportunities for all people, regardless of ethnicity or phenotypic variation. Earlier AAA resolutions against racism (1961, 1969, 1971, 1972) have spoken to this concern. The AAA further resolves: Whereas all human beings are members of one species, *Homo sapiens*, and, Whereas, differentiating species into biologically defined "races" has proven meaningless and unscientific as a way of explaining variation (whether in intelligence or other traits), Therefore, the American Anthropological Association urges the academy, our political leaders, and our communities to affirm, without distraction by *mistaken claims of racially determined intelligence* [italics added], the common stake in assuring equal opportunity, in respecting diversity, and in securing a harmonious quality of life for all people. (p. 3)

Why does psychology persist in maintaining a concept of race that anthropologists, geneticists, and evolutionary biologists reject as scientifically meaningless? Will the American Psychological Association ever adopt a similar resolution? If not, why not? If so, when?

10. From this, one can predict that the multitude of ethnic groups that were lumped together in the racial category Black to justify apartheid in South Africa will, within the next 20 years or so, assert their ethnicity and redefine themselves in terms of the many different ethnic groups to which they belong.

11. The earliest use of IQ and other mental tests to define ethnic groups as inferior races and exploit or exclude them involved not only African Americans, but also Native Americans and several European ethnic groups, such as Slavs, Poles, and Jews (see Gould, 1981). Such data support our view that, when Americans define an ethnic group as a race, psychological research on that group entails measuring their bodies, brains, and minds in an effort (usually successful)

to demonstrate that group's inferiority. The content and nature of research on an ethnic group is predicted by racial versus ethnic constructions.

12. For detailed, historical presentations of America's racializing of various ethnic groups and its disastrous social, human, and foreign policy consequences, see Gossett, 1965; Gould, 1981; Sinkler, 1972; Stanton, 1960; and Weston, 1972.

13. Deloria, Jr. (1983) stated,

Whites claiming Indian blood generally tend to reinforce mythical beliefs about Indians. All but one person I met who claimed Indian blood claimed it on their grandmother's side. I once did a projection backward and discovered that [this means that] evidently most tribes were entirely female for the first 300 years of white occupation. No one, it seemed, wanted to claim a male Indian forbearer.

It doesn't take much insight into racial attitudes to understand the real meaning of the Indian-grandmother complex that plagues certain whites. A male ancestor has too much of the aura of the savage warrior, the unknown primitive . . . to make him a respectable member of the family tree. But a young Indian princess? Ah, there was royalty for the taking. . . . And royalty has always been an unconscious but all-consuming goal of the European immigrant. . . . Why is a remote Indian princess grandmother so necessary for many whites? Is it because they are afraid of being classed as foreigners? Do they need some blood tie with the frontier and its dangers in order to experience what it means to be an American? [Or] is it an attempt to avoid facing the guilt they bear for the treatment of the Indian? (pp. 48-49)

14. *Imperialist nostalgia* refers to the yearning to return to one's fantasies about the past of those one has enslaved or exploited, as well as the desire to be one's fantasies about the present of those people, irrespective of exploited/enslaved ethnic group. Native American "princesses" of colonial America were raped and slaughtered. Those who look back and yearn for princesses in their family line do not desire this historical reality but instead desire their own fantasies. Likewise, Native Americans today by and large live in abject poverty, face extraordinary discrimination, as well as substandard educational and health facilities, and struggle to maintain their original languages and cultural practices. Those who want to be Native Americans do not want to be this reality either, but rather, long for contact with their own fantasies about and stereotypes of the exotic, primitive Indian (see hooks, 1992, for a general discussion of imperialist nostalgia and what she calls "eating the other").

15. That psychology alone (and not other disciplines) is the defender of race is so well-known that it was discussed in a recent (February 13, 1995) issue of *Newsweek*.

16. We also refer the reader to the February 13, 1995, issue of *Newsweek* titled "What Color is Black? Science, Politics and Racial Identity," for the arguments of other scientists against the concept of race. Their deconstructions of race (their strategy for dismantling race as a scientific concept and exposing it as a political construct) are in many ways similar to our own.

2

Toward a Theory
of African American Acculturation

In this chapter, we address the process of acculturation for African Americans and present a theoretical model of how such acculturation occurs. Here, as in the previous chapter, we are addressing acculturation at the individual level. Our interest is in differences among individual African Americans in the extent to which they participate in African American culture and in the role that such levels of acculturation play in African American behavior. This chapter and this book do not address acculturation at the larger, sociological level of analyzing the extent to and the process through which an entire ethnic group acculturates. At the larger sociological level, scholars debate the nature and stages of acculturation (assimilation in their terms) and whether assimilation is beneficial to ethnic minority groups, as well as to society (e.g., Gordon, 1964, 1978; Postiglione, 1983). This is not our interest. Rather, our focus is the fact that, whatever the general degree of acculturation of an entire ethnic group, some members within that group remain traditional (e.g., can speak only their native language), whereas others are highly acculturated (can speak only English and never learned the language of their culture). A strong relationship has been shown between these individual differences within an ethnic group in level of acculturation and behaviors such as smoking, experiencing psychiatric disorders, and seeking psychotherapy, as well as to health problems such as hypertension. This is our focus.

Likewise, then, we are not advocating the assimilation of (entire) ethnic minority groups nor addressing how that occurs.[1] Indeed, we are not even advocating the acculturation of individuals within an ethnic group, for whether that is psychologically beneficial or not is an empirical question, to be answered by empirical investigations. Instead, our focus is on these questions:

> How and why do some individuals remain traditional whereas others become acculturated?
> What kinds of variables predict those differences?
> Is acculturation a unidirectional process, a one-way street out of one's culture of origin, or is it more like a freeway loop that exits and then returns to one's culture of origin?
> What are the behavioral correlates of acculturation?

In this chapter, we address the first three theoretical questions. In the remaining chapters, we address the last question, the empirical question, through a series of empirical investigations.

We begin by examining existing theories of acculturation developed for other ethnic groups and by summarizing the major variables associated with acculturation for other ethnic minority groups. We then move to a theoretical exploration of acculturation among African Americans.

AFRICAN AMERICANS AND
EXISTING MODELS OF ACCULTURATION

As noted in the first chapter, theories of acculturation have by and large ignored African Americans, because African Americans are construed by psychology to be a cultureless race (Lambert & Taylor, 1990). Yet, issues of acculturation are as salient for (if not more salient for) African Americans as they are for new immigrants (Lambert & Taylor, 1990). Consequently, an abundance of evidence indicates that African Americans have very strong feelings about maintaining their cultural traditions. For example, Lambert and Taylor (1990) surveyed a large sample of African American parents and asked them if they believed that African Americans and other minorities should relinquish or should maintain their distinctive culture and its traditions. The researchers found that African American parents favored all ethnic groups maintaining their cultures; they favored cultural pluralism. These African American parents were specific about the aspects of African American culture that they deemed most important to maintain. The sample insisted that African Americans

> in general should keep their own styles of food, dress, music; that ethnic values dealing with childrearing and family relationships should be maintained; that courses about the cultural history of blacks should be taught in both community-run as well as public schools. (Lambert & Taylor, 1990, p. 137)

Lambert and Taylor's (1990) survey participants also endorsed maintaining African American language or dialect (Black English Vernacular, BEV) and cultural styles of communicating (e.g., testifyin'), particularly for "festivities, cultural activities, and religious services, and not only for conversations with older generation members, but for most communication within the family" (p. 138). The parents were well aware of the society's negative attitudes toward and misunderstanding of BEV (as broken English), and therefore they believed that Standard English should be spoken in school and to European Americans. Thus mastery of both BEV and Standard English (i.e., being bi-dialectical) was favored by these parents, more than was mastery of only one dialect. The negative attitudes of European Americans toward many aspects of African American culture (BEV, in particular) in part led Lambert and Taylor (1990) to conclude that issues of acculturation were perhaps even more central in the lives of African Americans than in the lives of new immigrants.

Like Lambert and Taylor (1990), we also hypothesize that acculturation is a central issue for African Americans. Nonetheless, the general models of acculturation ignore African Americans (as well as other old immigrants, such as Jews) and are based primarily on new immigrants. These models may not apply well to African Americans or to any other old (versus new) immigrant group as a result, and a new model may be needed to address issues of acculturation among African Americans.

There are many models of acculturation, that is, theories regarding the process and outcome of adaptation of ethnic minority individuals to a multicultural society in which their culture is one of many subcultures and is not the dominant culture (hence the term *minority*).[2] In a review of the literature on acculturation, LaFromboise, Coleman, and Gerton (1993) argued that these models could be grouped into four general types which they called assimilation, acculturation, alternation, and multiculturalism.

By *assimilation*, LaFromboise et al. (1993) refer to absorption into the dominant culture, the classic use of the term (Gordon, 1964). The assimilation model of acculturation argues that ethnic minorities adapt to a multicultural society by relinquishing their culture of origin in favor of the dominant culture. Assimilation is a unidirectional (one-way) process of adaptation, a one-way street away from the culture of origin, and its outcome is fully acculturated (assimilated) minorities. The problems inherent in assimilation are widely recognized as (a) rejection by the majority group, (b) rejection by the culture of origin, and (c) the stress of the process of assimilating. We can regard assimilation as an all-or-none model where the culture of origin is fully replaced by the dominant culture for the individual. In our theoretical model of African American acculturation, we refer to such individuals as *assimilated-acculturated*, to indicate that, for all intents and purposes, all major aspects of African American culture (the culture of origin) are absent from the individual's cultural-behavioral repertoire.

By *acculturation*, LaFromboise et al. (1993) refer to absorption into the dominant culture (assimilation), but with some important aspects of the culture of origin retained. The acculturation model assumes that minorities adapt to a multicultural society by relinquishing most but not all of their culture of origin. Acculturation also is a unidirectional process (a one-way street away from the culture of origin), and its outcome is highly acculturated minorities. The acculturation model is an almost all-or-none model, where the culture of origin is almost fully replaced by the dominant culture. In our theoretical model of African American acculturation, we refer to these individuals as *highly acculturated*, to indicate that many but not all important aspects of African American culture are absent from the individual's cultural-behavioral repertoire.

By *alternation*, LaFromboise et al. (1993) refer to an additive model of acculturation in which the dominant culture is added to the culture of origin so that individuals participate in two cultural traditions. This model assumes that minorities adapt to a multicultural society by adding the society's dominant culture to their cultural-behavioral repertoire. The outcome of alternation is bicultural minorities.

All alternation models assume that minorities are necessarily bicultural. Some of these models argue that this biculturalism consists of alternating (switching) from one cultural repertoire to another; these models argue that individuals exhibit the behavioral repertoire of their culture of origin in some settings and of the dominant culture in others. Other models argue that this biculturalism consists of selecting some aspects of the culture of origin (e.g., religion, music, foods) and some aspects of the dominant culture (e.g., speech, values), with this new mix or sum constituting one's cultural-behavioral repertoire (see LaFromboise et al., 1993). In our model of African American acculturation, we refer to those who alternate between two well-developed, distinctly different, cultural-behavioral repertoires as *alternating-bicultural*. Those who have selected aspects of their culture of origin and of the dominant culture and blended these into a single, unified cultural-behavioral repertoire are referred to in our model as *blended-bicultural*.

Finally, by *multiculturalism*, LaFromboise et al. (1993) refer to alternation models that assume that more than two cultures are involved. Although each of these models accounts for some of the empirical evidence on acculturation (see LaFromboise et al., 1993), we believe that none of these models alone is sufficient to describe acculturation among African Americans. For example, some African Americans are assimilated and could be understood in terms of the assimilation model. Other African Americans are highly acculturated and could be understood in terms of the models that LaFromboise et al. (1993) called acculturation models. Still other African Americans are alternating biculturals who switch from cultural repertoire to cultural repertoire, much like multiple personalities, and who experience what W. E. B. DuBois (1961) long ago called the "double consciousness" (the awareness of the two repertoires). Still others are what we have called blended-biculturals, and no doubt also experience the double-consciousness, although they do not engage in radical alternation and culture switching. But none of these models alone describes the diversity of levels and types of acculturation among African Americans.

In addition, because these models are based on new immigrants, they assume that members of an ethnic-minority group begin their lives as traditional and then become bicultural or acculturated. We suggest, however, that members of an ethnic-minority group may not begin their lives as traditional but instead could begin from the starting point of acculturated or bicultural, if their parents were acculturated or bicultural; this certainly is the case for many African Americans. Yet, changes in the cultural alignment of these individuals no doubt occur as well, and those have not been addressed. Indeed, unlike other models of acculturation, ours hypothesizes that people can change from acculturated to traditional (neotraditional, we call them). Whereas other models tend to assume that the direction of change is always away from the culture of origin, we hypothesize that for many minorities, the direction of change often is away from the dominant culture (acculturated or bicultural) and back to immersion in the culture of origin (neo-traditional). Unlike other models, ours holds that acculturation can go in any direction and that its direction is more often backward (a return to traditional) or circular (from traditional to acculturated and then back to traditional). We hypothesize that this latter process occurs for many African Americans (as well as for other old immigrant groups) and that acculturation is far more complex than current models imply.

In addition to these general models of acculturation, researchers have identified variables that play a role in acculturation among new immigrants. These are (a) contact with (exposure to) the dominant culture and the extent (length) of that contact, (b) age and gender at the time of contact with/exposure to the dominant culture, and (c) treatment by that culture (see LaFromboise et al., 1993, for a review of these variables). It is difficult to know what role these variables play in acculturation among African Americans, or indeed among other old immigrant groups (e.g., Italians, Irish, Jews, Poles).

With the major models of and variables associated with acculturation outlined, we can turn now to a theoretical model of acculturation among African Americans.

A THEORETICAL MODEL OF
AFRICAN AMERICAN ACCULTURATION

We begin by outlining four basic concepts that are integral to this discussion: duplicate institutions, ethnic enclaves (communities), ethnic parent-group, and ethnic socialization. These concepts probably apply generally to all ethnic minority groups.

BASIC CONCEPTS

Duplicate Institutions

We have defined ethnic-minority groups as cultural groups whose culture is not the dominant one in a multicultural society. We can state further that, in general, all ethnic-minority cultures function as semiautonomous entities or subcultures within the larger common culture in that each possesses its own *analogous, parallel, noncomplementary (yet duplicate) institutions* (van den Berghe, 1978). These duplicate institutions include the ethnic group's own newspapers, magazines, churches, schools, nightclubs, clinics or hospitals, social and political clubs and organizations, leaders, indigenous healers, restaurants, stores, and the like. All ethnic minority cultures are characterized by the presence of such duplicate institutions; the presence of numerous, culturally specific sets of duplicate institutions (e.g., for Jews, Latinos, and other groups) defines a society as multicultural, as culturally pluralistic. These duplicate institutions reflect and maintain each minority culture and so are essential to the perpetuation of the ethnic group's culture and identity. The existence of such duplicate institutions for African Americans is obvious and undeniable, and it is evidence for the existence of an African American culture.

Members of ethnic groups acquire and maintain their culture through these institutions and through their families. That is, members of an ethnic-minority group learn (acquire and are reinforced for using) a culturally specific behavioral and cognitive repertoire. These parallel, segmented institutions are most prevalent (and influential) in ethnic enclaves, the second feature exhibited by ethnic minority groups or cultures.

Ethnic Enclaves

Ethnic enclaves refers to voluntary or involuntary physical and spatial segregation and concentration (i.e., territorial propinquity; van den Berghe, 1978) of members of an ethnic group in geographically distinct, more or less ethnically homogenous neighborhoods or communities. The tendency to live, work, and/or spend leisure time in ethnic enclaves is the result of discrimination, as well as of choice and preference. Several of these enclaves may exist for each ethnic group, these may differ by socioeconomic status, and they may be widely dispersed geographically (e.g., on the East and the West coasts). Contact among enclaves is maintained through newspapers, magazines, political organizations, and informal networks, as well as through individuals who have friends or relatives in another enclave or who have themselves moved from one enclave to another. Such contact assures consistency of cultural socialization across enclaves and thus of the repertoire of behaviors acquired and maintained. Thus African American culture, like other minority cultures, is characterized by a multitude of African American enclaves or communities. Migration patterns for many African Americans, like other ethnic-minorities, consist of moving from one established enclave to another. We refer to African American (or other minority) enclaves as the *minority local environment* and refer to enclaves of the dominant cultural group as the *dominant local environment*.

In addition, irrespective of the socioeconomic status of an enclave, these enclaves are most prototypical of the culture and are essential to its maintenance, to the extent that they are replete with the aforementioned duplicate cultural institutions and associated cultural practices. There is considerable migration into and out of these enclaves, with new members (e.g., those from the home country) typically migrating to a well-established enclave. Thus African American duplicate institutions tend to be located in the various African American communities (enclaves) in the country; these communities are prototypical of the culture and have contact with each other. In these communities, cultural practices regarding diet, childrearing, music, language, religion, health, and social interaction are seen in their most unadulterated form.

The cognitive and behavioral repertoire acquired through sociali-zation within enclaves is culturally specific. People socialized within enclaves have acquired the behaviors, ways of under-standing, taxonomies, interactional rules, dialect, and cognitive schema specific to their culture through cultural and *ethnic socialization*. Thus individual African Americans (like individual Latinos) who spend most of their lives in and are socialized in ethnically homogenous communities (enclaves) tend to be the most prototypical (traditional) members of their culture. The best predictor of level of acculturation is where a person lives and spends most of his/her time.

These geographically and culturally sequestered ethnic enclaves are characterized by (a) a high degree of interaction among members of the group; (b) infrequent contact with the dominant group and little interest in or internalization of its culture; and (c) friendships and kin relations (however constructed) by and large restricted to the ethnic-cultural group, with a tendency toward endogamy (marriage within the cultural group) as well. These three features of enclaves perpetuate the culture of the ethnic group. Thus African Americans who have spent most of their lives in well-established, more or less ethnically homo-genous African American communities tend to interact primarily with other African Americans and rarely with European Ameri-cans (except perhaps at and related to work); to have internalized little of the dominant culture; to have friends, social support networks, and marriage partners within their ethnic group.

Ethnic enclaves have considerable resources (reinforcers) that are made available to those who have lived in the enclave for a long time. Such resources include social support, money, goods, services, influential contacts, and the like. Such resources are most available to those who live within or maintain close contact with the enclave, because the amount of resources allocated to people in need is contingent upon the amount that they have contributed (Stack, 1974).

Parent Groups

Those who live their entire lives within ethnic enclaves and never leave, and whose parents and grandparents also did so, are a special group of the highly traditional that we refer to as the *parent group*. These individuals are the most traditional (prototypical) members of the culture; they retain the oldest of traditions, practices, and beliefs, as well as, in many cases, the original language of the ethnic group, and they tend to be the well-respected elders of the community. They are the guardians, the sentinels of the culture. A few members of the parent group (those whose families have lived within the enclave for several generations) wield considerable decision-making power (where enclavewide decisions and the allocation of the enclave's resources are concerned), and they possess a high degree of prestige and authority. Members of parent groups constitute what Portes (1984) called the power circles within ethnic minority communities.

The parent group never acculturates. This group of staunchly traditional, elder members of an ethnic-minority culture remains culturally stable because its members have no reason to believe that acculturation entails any benefits that they cannot accrue within the enclave, and because their lives are restricted to the enclave. Rather than changing any of their "old ways," they lament the extent to which the young deviate from the traditions and values of the culture of origin.

Finally, the political leaders of an ethnic-minority community (those who lead and organize interactions with the dominant group on behalf of the minority group) do not generally come from this parent group, but they could not operate without the parent group's support. Rather, the leaders of an ethnic minority group tend to be highly acculturated members who have, after experiencing considerable discrimination, returned to their communities with a new and deeper sense of cultural awareness and pride (for examples of this in a diversity of ethnic-minority groups, see Breton, 1978; Esman, 1987; Neilsen, 1986; and Portes, 1984). Thus mobilization of an ethnic-minority community for political action is more likely to be led by these newly returned, young, acculturated members than by "older members, less acculturated . . . and more restricted to ethnic enclaves" (Lambert & Taylor, 1990, p. 34). The circular nature of acculturation, the pattern of traditional → bicultural → acculturated → neotraditional, is an important source of leaders.

Ethnic Socialization

Finally, racial socialization refers to messages about African Americans, Whites, and the status of African Americans vis-à-vis Whites that are communicated and taught to children (see, for example, Dembo & Hughes, 1990; Harrison, Wilson, Pine, Chan, & Buriel, 1990; Peters, 1985; Thompson, 1994). Among other things, these messages address racism and racial barriers. We hypothesize that such socialization occurs for all ethnic-minority groups and that the messages entailed are similar. Here we refer to this more general phenomenon as *ethnic socialization* and define it as follows:

Ethnic socialization refers to socialization that focuses on (a) the nature and meaning of being a member of an ethnic-minority group; (b) the relative status of one's ethnic-minority group vis-à-vis the dominant cultural group; (c) the discrimination and unfair, hostile treatment that the individual can expect to experience as a consequence of being a member of an ethnic-minority group; and (d) explanations of the dominant group's discrimination and hostility—causal attributions regarding racism.

We hypothesize that such ethnic socialization occurs for the members of any minority group that experiences considerable discrimination, that it occurs early in life (e.g., when the child enters school), and that parental figures may believe that such socialization is necessary to prepare their child for a biased, discriminatory, and unfair world. Most important, we hypothesize that the nature of the causal, explanatory attributions regarding racism plays a major role in the nature and outcome of acculturation. Specifically, we hypothesize that ethnic-minority parental figures communicate one of these explanations for the dominant group's behavior:

The dominant group is all bad.   All members of the dominant group are ethnocentric and racist; all are biased against our ethnic group; all can be expected to treat you in a hostile or discriminatory manner, and therefore none of them is to be trusted. They discriminate against you because that is their nature and is the nature of things; they cannot change, and intergroup relations cannot change.

The dominant group is composed of individuals who differ significantly in their biases against members of our ethnic group. Some members of the dominant group will discriminate against you and treat you in a hostile manner, and others will treat you as fairly as they know how. Those who discriminate against you do so because they lack intelligence or lack information (they are ignorant), whereas those who treat you fairly do so because they are intelligent and can learn to treat you in a fully nondiscriminatory manner. Intergroup relations can change with increased information, education, and intercultural knowledge.

The dominant group is all good.   Members of the dominant group are more cultured, sophisticated, normal, mature, and intelligent than members of our ethnic group (who are, with a few exceptions, All Bad). Some members of the dominant group may discriminate against you because they perceive you as being like the rest of our basically All Bad group. You must demonstrate that you are not like other members of our group, that you are an exception. When that is clear to the dominant group, then all members of the dominant group will treat you fairly.

As we argue below, these three ethnic socialization messages have very different implications for the nature, speed, and outcome of acculturation.

With these basic concepts in hand, we can turn to the process of acculturation among African Americans. The theoretical principles and processes advanced here stem from our observations of African Americans; they also may apply to other old immigrant groups.

PRINCIPLES OF
AFRICAN AMERICAN ACCULTURATION

THE PRINCIPLE OF RETURN

Acculturation is a dynamic, dialectical, and/or circular process, in the sense that all members invariably and inevitably return to the values, traditions, and practices of their culture of origin—and many may return to live in an ethnic enclave, as well. We refer to those who return to the values and traditions of their culture of origin as *neotraditional* to distinguish them from *traditional* members, who always have been traditional. Whatever an individual's initial level of acculturation, and no matter how acculturated or bicultural he or she may have become in the course of his or her life, all members of minority groups are neotraditional by the end of the lives. There are three reasons that all individuals return to the culture of origin. These are age, children, and racism and discrimination faced in dominant-group local environments.

Age. With increasing age, acculturated and bicultural people experience a sense of loss regarding the extent to which they have departed from the practices, values, and traditions of the culture of origin. A nostalgic love for and pride in the "old neighborhood" or the "old country" and one's roots arises. Others experience a renewed need for a sense of roots as they look back on their lives and ask themselves who they are and who they have been. Still others feel that they are alone and adrift with their self-made values and practices—they feel that something is missing—and they long for a stable, enduring set of traditions. For others, the desire to return is prompted by impending death; they feel the need to mend old wounds, resolve old debates and feuds, establish peace and harmony with the family, and reimmerse themselves in the church so that their funeral can be sanctioned and attended by established, religious elders.

Children. As children are born, the acculturated and bicultural experience a duty to educate them about the culture of origin (about their roots) and to assure that they have adequate knowledge of the culture's practices and beliefs, as well as contact with grandparents and other family members who may be very traditional. Alternatively, many acculturated people, experiencing a sense of loss of a solid, cultural community, regret their acculturation and do not wish their children to experience the same fate. For either of these reasons, then, and paradoxically, acculturated parents often purposefully raise their children to be highly traditional. Alternatively, the children of acculturated and bicultural parents may themselves initiate discussion of the culture of origin and demand to have contact with and more thorough knowledge of it, as they attempt to establish their own cultural identities. The children may thereby initiate parental return to the culture of origin.

Racism/discrimination. Acculturated and bicultural people, who have abandoned "their internal colonies, neighborhoods, and enclaves" to work with and compete with the dominant group in dominant local environments, invariably experience a new "awareness of racial and cultural differences" (Portes, 1984, p. 385). Ethnicity becomes salient for them because of the racism and discrimination they face in the dominant local environment. In addition, because they are often the sole minority (or one of a few minorities) in the dominant local environment, their ethnic group membership increases in salience for them and for members of the dominant group. Inevitably and paradoxically, then, those who spend most of their time in dominant local environments are most keenly aware of their ethnic identity and its social meanings. These individuals invariably return to the culture of origin, to its values and traditions and practices, as the neotraditional leaders and activists of the community (Breton, 1978; Esman, 1987; Portes, 1984). Unlike the truly traditional, who are traditional because they know no culture but their own, the neotraditional—and particularly those who return because of discrimination—know the dominant culture well and consciously reject it. They regret the path they once chose and believe that acculturation was not "worth it." Some of these neotraditionals become self-righteously traditional, for they are not simply immersing themselves in the culture of origin but simultaneously are rejecting the dominant culture: They (rather than the truly traditional members of the parent group) may adopt African clothing and names, learn an African language, visit African nations, and move back to an enclave; their adherence to tradition has a conscious, deliberate quality lacking among the truly traditional, for whom immersion in the culture of origin is the only life they know.

Any one or combination of these three variables may account for an individual's return to origin. The principle of return is seen in each individual over time (developmentally) as well as in families across generations, whether the initial starting point for person or family is traditional, bicultural, or acculturated. With the exception of those who remain traditional their entire lives, each individual can be characterized by each level of acculturation at some point—each person experiences them all, as shown in Table 2.1.

The principle of return predicts that differences in levels of acculturation will not necessarily coincide with differences in social class (income) or education; traditional African Americans can be rich or poor, with little education or a great deal. So can highly acculturated African Americans. This is because those who become highly acculturated and acquire college educations and high incomes inevitably return to traditionality (neotraditionality), such that traditional people vary considerably in education and

TABLE 2.1 The Principle of Return

Initial Level of Acculturation	Intermediate Levels of Acculturation		Final Level of Acculturation
Pre-Adulthood (Ages 0-22)	Early Adulthood (Ages 18-39)	Midlife Transition (Ages 35-50)	Late Adulthood (Ages 50+)
Traditional	Bicultural	Acculturated ↔ Bicultural	Neotraditional
Bicultural	Acculturated	Bicultural ↔ Neotraditional	Neotraditional
Acculturated	Acculturated	Bicultural ↔ Neotraditional	Neotraditional
Traditional	Marginal	Marginal ↔ Neotraditional	Neotraditional
Traditional	Bicultural	Bicultural ↔ Neotraditional	Neotraditional
Traditional	Traditional	Traditional ↔ Traditional	Traditional

income. In addition, of course, those who acquire a college education and greater subsequent incomes do not necessarily acculturate. Many attend traditional Black colleges and remain traditional throughout their lives, such that education and income are not related to traditionality. Likewise, highly acculturated people are not necessarily highly educated, as discussed below.

*The Principle of
Fractionization and Allopatricity*

Acculturation proceeds by *fractionization*, the splitting off of an individual or a family (a fraction) from the values and traditions represented by the parent group and other traditional members of the culture. Acculturation is not the slow, steady transformation of the parent group or of the entire culture; rather, it is the rapid transformation of fractions, of small, somewhat deviant and/or culturally isolated individuals and families. Like evolution, acculturation proceeds through the rapid fractionization of "small, peripheral isolates—rather than by slow change in large, central populations" (Gould, 1977, p. 62).

Fractionization occurs through *allopatricity* (*allopatric* means in another place). The members of the culture who are most likely to acculturate are less traditional than most members of the culture. They are culturally and perhaps (but not necessarily) also geographically in another place. They differ somewhat from the traditional person, and everyone knows that they are different. They don't participate in many of the culture's practices or language use or social activities; they are on the margins of the culture. If both parents are African Americans, an individual's allopatricity may be due to (a) early (childhood) positive experiences with and exposure to the dominant group; (b) frequent contact with the dominant group through work, school, or living in an integrated neighborhood; (c) frequent negative experiences with own cultural group and community; and/or (d) being selected by the family as the individual who will acculturate, and then being punished for culturally specific behaviors (e.g., language and speech, clothing). Where both parents are not African American, allopatricity can be a function of mixed ethnicity (e.g., Black/Hmong, Black/Latino, Black/White) or of being raised by non-African American adoptive parents.

In any event, those who are not quite full, traditional members of the culture—who are in another place—are most likely to acculturate. We can think of these people as prepared to acculturate, as ready for the process. Other individuals also can acculturate, of course, but the more traditional they are, the more difficult, timely, and stressful the process of acculturation is. Acculturation is a less difficult and faster process for those who are prepared. This is because those who are prepared already deviate from the traditional center of the culture and thereby have a smaller cultural distance to traverse to acculturate. The distance between their cultural repertoires and that of the dominant culture is small. By definition, the distance between their own culture and the dominant culture is greatest for those who are traditional. The absolute value of the change necessary to acculturate decreases as initial traditionality decreases.

The Principle of Quality of Contact

In order to acculturate, individuals inevitably must have extended contact with the dominant cultural group. Whether this contact starts out as primarily positive or primarily negative in part predicts the nature, speed, and path of the acculturative process.

THE PRINCIPLE OF ETHNIC SOCIALIZATION

Finally, the content of the message that individuals have learned about the dominant group (described earlier) also predicts the nature, speed, and path of the acculturative process. These principles are detailed in Table 2.2

As indicated in Table 2.2, the message of ethnic socialization, as well as the nature of the initial prolonged contact with the dominant group, predicts the outcome of the acculturative process. We hypothesize that *acculturative stress* only occurs for those for whom the ethnic socialization message does not match their initial experiences. The terms *alternating-bicultural, blended-bicultural, traditional,* and *neotraditional* have been defined earlier in the chapter. By the term *marginal*, we mean individuals who have rejected both African American culture (their culture of origin) *and* the dominant culture. We hypothesize that marginal African Americans are those who are most likely to become drug abusers and criminals, because they have not internalized the values of any culture; this hypothesis is consistent with the available empirical evidence on the topic (e.g., Oetting & Beauvais, 1990-1991; Oetting, Edwards, & Beauvais, 1989).

PROCESSES IN
AFRICAN AMERICAN ACCULTURATION

With the above principles in mind, how exactly does acculturation happen? We hypothesize that the actual how of acculturation is a function of *social comparison* processes (Festinger, 1954):

Social comparison is a process in which people compare themselves to others in a situation to evaluate the extent to which their behaviors and responses are acceptable, where *acceptable* means that responses and behaviors will be reinforced (with

TABLE 2.2 Role of Ethnic Socialization in Acculturation of Traditional People

Ethnic Socialization Message	Initial Prolonged Contact	Immediate Outcome	Intermediate Levels of Acculturation
Dominant group is all bad	Positive →	Acculturative stress →	Alternating-bicultural or marginal
	Negative →	Failed acculturation →	Traditional
		Slow acculturation →	Alternating-bicultural
Dominant group includes individuals	Positive →	Rapid acculturation →	Assimilated-acculturated or blended-bicultural
	Negative →	Rapid acculturation →	Alternating-bicultural or blended-bicultural
Dominant group is all good	Positive →	Rapid acculturation	Assimilated-acculturated or blended-bicultural
		Acculturative stress →	Marginal
	Negative →	Failed acculturation →	Traditional

smiles, praise, liking, money, job offers) or punished (through ignoring, distancing, excluding). African Americans become acculturated or bicultural by comparing themselves to the dominant group in a dominant local environment to appraise the extent to which their behavioral repertoire is acceptable within that dominant local environment. Behaviors (e.g., interactional styles, opinions) and stimuli (e.g., clothing, makeup) common among the dominant group become discriminative stimuli signaling that reinforcement is coming (S^Ds), whereas behaviors and stimuli absent among the dominant group but present for the acculturating minority person become discriminative stimuli indicating that punishment is coming ($S\Delta$s). New behaviors specific to the dominant group and acquired through social comparison processes (and modeling) may be blended into one's existing repertoire (blended-bicultural), may replace one's existing repertoire (assimilated-acculturated), or may be added to one's existing repertoire and engaged in only when in dominant local environments (alternating-bicultural).

Many aspects of this theoretical model of the process and stages of acculturation are empirically testable; we invite and encourage such research. The model will not be tested here because it requires a longitudinal study. That is, to demonstrate the principle of return, for example, one would need to follow a large sample of African Americans (who differ by age) for 10 to 20 years and assess their levels of acculturation annually. Such an investigation is beyond the scope and purpose of this book. Instead, we turn now to the development of the African American Acculturation Scale (AAAS) and to studies of the relationship between scores on it and African American behavior. As will be seen, the AAAS only measures the extent to which an individual is immersed in African American culture or not. Very high scores on the AAAS indicate a person who is very traditional, and very low scores, a person who is highly acculturated. It is not possible to know precisely what scores in the midrange mean. In addition, the AAAS does not measure aspects of European American culture, and as far as we know, there is no such thing as the

European American Acculturation Scale (EAAS). Consequently, some aspects of this theoretical model cannot be tested until an EAAS is developed. Those who score equally high on the AAAS and the fictitious EAAS would be classified as bicultural, whereas those who score very low on both would be classified as marginal. Because *the AAAS, as will be seen, only measures degrees of immersion in African American culture,* we can only compare the highly acculturated to the highly traditional and cannot address biculturalism or multiculturalism or the meaning of midrange scores on the scale.

NOTES

1. We can state, however, that pluralism (the existence of many different cultures) rather than assimilation describes American society (Lambert & Taylor, 1990). Our nation, like others (e.g., Canada), does not consist of ethnic groups who have relinquished their cultures and "melted" into a larger cultural whole; instead, it consists of "unmeltable ethnics" (Novak's 1972 term) who have maintained their cultures. We support such pluralism and believe that a peaceful pluralistic (multicultural) society can exist. In Canada, this has been accomplished through federal policies that assure the economic security of each ethnic group and support and maintain each group's ethnic identity and distinct culture. Canada has found that these federal policies, rather than increasing intergroup conflict, have decreased such conflict and increased intergroup appreciation, to yield a cohesive mosaic (Berry, Kalin, & Taylor, 1977; Lambert, Mermigis, & Taylor, 1986; Lambert & Taylor, 1990). Supporting cultural differences (rather than imposing assimilation) appears to be the key to intergroup cooperation.

2. The term *ethnic minority* refers to cultural groups (ethnics) whose culture is not the dominant one in a society (minority).

3

Development and Cross-Validation of
the African American Acculturation Scale
(AAAS)

THEORETICAL BASIS OF ITEMS

Acculturation scales for other ethnic groups (discussed in Chapter 1) typically assess many different aspects or dimensions of the culture in question. We modeled the African American Acculturation Scale (AAAS) after those scales and thus constructed items to assess a diversity of aspects of African American culture. Of the many aspects of a culture that could be included in any acculturation scale, we selected the eight dimensions described below, after a careful examination of the empirical evidence on African American culture. Items assessing each dimension were structured so that higher scores (high agreement with the item) indicated a more traditional cultural orientation and lower scores (low agreement with the item) indicated a more acculturated (less traditional) cultural orientation.

1. *Traditional African American Family Structures and Practices* (Family; 19 items). Several items included in the scale were designed to assess aspects of the traditional African American family and traditional practices regarding the family. Many items assessed child taking, child-keeping, or informal adoption. This practice may have predated slavery; it may have been common in the African societies that regard children as the offspring of the community as a whole (Shimkin, Shimkin, & Frate, 1978). Informal adoption persisted throughout slavery as slaves "took in" (informally adopted) slave children whose parents were sold away or killed; they also adopted adult and (particularly) elderly slaves who needed a home and care (Boyd-Franklin, 1989a). Such informal adoptions have persisted since slavery; African American families continue to informally adopt children and adults who need a home (Boyd-Franklin, 1989a; Hill, 1977; Stack, 1974).

Other items were designed to assess the extended family (e.g., a household may include aunts, uncles, cousins, and grandparents) that was common among the Africans who became slaves (Shimkin et al., 1978), persisted throughout slavery, and remains common among contemporary African Americans (Barnes, 1981; Hays, 1973; Shimkin et al., 1978). Additional items assessed African American familism (the belief that the family's needs take priority over those of the individual) and deep respect for elders (Boyd-Franklin, 1989a; Carter & Helms, 1987). Some items assessed co-sleeping and co-bathing (i.e., children sleep and bathe with other children or with an adult). These practices are common among African American families (Lozoff, Wolf, & Davis, 1984; Ward, 1971), as well as among families in other cultures, such as Japan (Caudill & Plath, 1966) and Mexico (Morelli, Rogoff, Oppenheim, & Goldsmith, 1992); they are rare among European Americans, when compared to African Americans (Crowell, Keener, Ginsburg, & Anders, 1987; Lozoff et al., 1984; Mandansky

& Edelbrock, 1990; Whiting & Edwards, 1988). Examples of items in this subscale are the following:

> When I was young, I shared a bed at night with my sister, brother, or some other relative.
> It's best to try to move your whole family ahead in this world than it is to be out for only yourself.

Theoretically, traditional African Americans are more likely to have participated in informal adoption and co-sleeping (for example) than acculturated African Americans, who are more like European Americans and, like European Americans, do not engage in such practices.

2. *Preference for Things African American* (Preferences; 24 items). Items here were meant to assess preference for African American newspapers, magazines, music, games, and for African American people as well. Examples of items are as follows:

> I know how to play bid whist.
> Most of the music I listen to is by Black artists.
> I read (or used to read) *Essence* or *Ebony* magazine.
> Most of my friends are Black.

Theoretically, traditional African Americans (like the traditional members of any other ethnic minority group) should show more of a preference for their own culture's music, newspapers, arts, and people than acculturated African Americans, and so the former should score higher than the latter.

3. *Preparation and Consumption of Traditional Foods* (Foods; 17 items). These included items such as the following:

> Sometimes I eat collard greens.
> Sometimes I cook ham hocks.

Theoretically, traditional African Americans are more likely than acculturated ones to consume and prepare traditional cultural foods. More acculturated African Americans, like European Americans, are theoretically unlikely to eat such foods.

4. *Interracial Attitudes/Cultural Mistrust* (Attitudes; 33 items). Items here were designed to assess attitudes about European Americans and their institutions that are somewhat common among African Americans; such attitudes have been assessed empirically in previous studies, where they were called *cultural mistrust* (Terrell & Terrell, 1981). Items included,

> I don't trust most White people.
> IQ tests were set up purposefully to discriminate against Black people.
> Deep in their hearts, most White people are racists.

As previously, higher scores (greater agreement with) these items indicates a more traditional cultural orientation. Theoretically, such beliefs are common among traditional African Americans but not among more acculturated or bicultural ones.

5. *Traditional African American Health Beliefs and Practices* (Health; 36 items). These items were designed to assess contemporary African American health beliefs and practices that stem from the West African cultures of the slaves and persisted through slavery to the present (Mbiti, 1975). These include the belief that minor illness has natural causes and cures, whereas major illness has supernatural (or "unnatural") causes and cures (Landrine & Klonoff, 1992; Mbiti, 1975). Questions also assessed the tendency to rely on traditional, indigenous healers (ministers, root doctors) who use religious ritual, herbs, and roots as cures today, just as their forefathers and mothers did during and before slavery (Jackson, 1981). Specific questions involved the older, African American woman indigenous healer who is popular in the African American community (Bailey, 1991; Jackson, 1981; Jordan, 1975, 1979). This role began with the African American woman "slave doctor," whose preslavery knowledge of the use of herbs made her largely responsible for the health of the slaves (Goodson, 1987). Traditional health practices involving teas or prayer, these being common in much of the African American

community (see Bailey, 1987; Hill, 1973, 1976; Scott, 1974; Snow, 1974, 1977), also were assessed. Other items assessed the use of or belief in rootwork and voodoo, which has persisted among some African Americans since slavery (Baer, 1985; Hall & Bourne, 1973; Snow, 1978). Finally, some items assessed knowledge of and experience with the African American folk disorder (culture-bound syndrome) known as "falling out" (see Weidman, 1979). Some examples of items are,

> Some old Black women/ladies know how to cure disease.
> I believe that some people know how to use voodoo.
> Prayer can cure disease.
> I have "fallen out."
> If doctors can't cure you, you should try going to a root doctor or to your minister.

Theoretically, traditional African Americans should indicate more agreement with these cultural beliefs and practices than acculturated African Americans, who, like European Americans, should reject these in favor of Western biomedical views.

6. *Traditional African American Religious Beliefs and Practices* (Religion; 12 items). Several items written for the scale assessed the deep spirituality that permeated all aspects of African life (Nobles, 1980), persisted among the slaves despite attempts of slave masters to destroy it (Nobles, 1980), and remains a major aspect of African American personality, culture, and community (McAdoo, 1981; Pipes, 1981). Such spirituality may entail extensive involvement in an African American church (Frazier, 1963), or it may be reflected in deep convictions, rather than church attendance. Examples of such items are,

> I believe in the Holy Ghost.
> I am a very religious person.

Traditional African Americans are, theoretically, more spiritual than acculturated African Americans (who are more like European

Americans) and so the former should score higher (agree) with these items.

7. *Traditional African American Childhood Socialization* (Childhood; 17 items). Items here were meant to assess the most common experiences of African American children, including playing African American games such as tonk and jumping double-dutch; growing up in an African American community; and singing in the church choir as a child. Examples of items are,

> When I was a child, I used to play tonk.
> When I was young, I was a member of a Black church.

Traditional African Americans, theoretically, are more likely to have played African American games and to have grown up in an African American neighborhood (enclave) than acculturated African Americans, who are more like European Americans and, as such, may have grown up in integrated or White neighborhoods and never participated in typical African American children's games and activities.

8. *Superstitions* (31 items). These items were meant to assess old superstitious beliefs that many African Americans were taught by their grandparents and whose historical origins appear to be ancient (former) cultural practices. Items included,

> You should never put a hat on a bed.
> I eat Black-eyed peas on New Year's Eve (for luck).

The first item, for example, appears to stem from the ancient practice of voodoo among the slaves and freed slaves, in which a hat was placed upon a person's bed to warn him that maintaining his present course of action would be met by a curse, hex, or other negative reaction. Highly traditional African Americans might hold these cultural superstitions (extinct cultural practices), whereas more acculturated African Americans, like European Americans, would not.

Thus, the items for each of the eight subscales were constructed so that high scores are equivalent to a traditional, cultural orientation (immersed in own culture) and low scores to a more acculturated orientation (not immersed in own culture). The meaning of scores in the midrange cannot be ascertained.

The authors developed several items reflecting the above eight dimensions of African American culture. In addition, seven African Americans from diverse geographical regions (e.g., New York City, Atlanta) were asked to generate their own lists of beliefs, practices, rituals, foods, games, and superstitions held by African Americans but not by European Americans and unknown to European Americans. Any item listed by at least three people (including the researchers) was included in the scale. The resulting original version of the AAAS consisted of 189 items (assessing eight subscales), to be rated on scales that ranged from 1 = *I totally disagree, this is not at all true of me* to 7 = *I totally agree, this is absolutely true of me.* This version of the scale was distributed.

STUDY 1

PARTICIPANTS

A questionnaire was completed by 183 adults (Sample 1), including 118 African Americans, 37 European Americans, 13 Latinos, 10 Asian Americans, and 5 people of mixed African American heritage (e.g., African American and Mexican American); the latter were included in the African American group in statistical analyses. The participants ranged in age from 15 to 72 years, with the average age being 32.81 years (Mode = 25 years, σ = 11.22 years); 51 were men and 132 were women. Their education levels were diverse: 32 had not completed high school; 25 were high school graduates; 74 had some college and 13 had graduated college; and 17 had master's or doctorate degrees. The geographical region of origin of the African American subjects was assessed to assure that the majority of the subjects were not from the Deep South. Results revealed that about half of the participants (59) were born in California, whereas the remainder (64) were born elsewhere; only 20 of the 123 African Americans had been born in the South.

PROCEDURE

The participants were approached in community organizations and drop-in centers in South Central Los Angeles, San Bernardino County, California, and Westchester County, New York, and asked to complete an anonymous Beliefs and Attitudes survey. An additional 100 questionnaires were distributed at the meeting of the American Psychological Association (APA) Minority Fellowship Program during the August 1993 APA Convention in Toronto. These questionnaires were accompanied by a brief letter explaining the purpose of the study, and self-addressed, stamped envelopes were provided for their return; 19 of these were returned (19% response rate). This assured that a small group of African Americans with very high levels of education would be included in the sample. A sheet requesting demographic data on participants constituted the last page of the questionnaire and included questions on the subject's age, ethnicity, income, work status, education level, state and city of birth, state and city of current residence, marital status, social class of family of origin, and other factors.

RESULTS

Preliminary Analyses for Item Retention

A preliminary series of multivariate analyses of variance (MANOVAs, not shown here) were conducted to assess the extent to which African Americans ($n = 123$) scored differently from non-African Americans (all other ethnic groups combined, $n = 60$) on the initial 189 items. Although the sample sizes for these analyses were small (about 10 subjects per variable), they were sufficient for the purpose of excluding items. Items on which African Americans differed from non-African Americans at the .05 level were retained, and items on which they did not were excluded. Fifty-seven items were dropped because they did not discriminate between African Americans and non-African Americans. The remaining 132 items were then examined to assess the extent to which African Americans agreed with them (rated the item 4 or higher on the 7-point scales). Although the previous analyses indicated that African Americans had expressed significantly greater agreement than European Americans with all 132 items, most African Americans may not have agreed much with the item nonetheless; for example, African Americans could have rated an item 3, this being higher than the rating of 1 from other ethnic groups, but with African Americans not agreeing much with the item. Thus, items on which 50% of African Americans agreed (a rating of 4 or higher) were retained, and all others were excluded. An additional 58 items were dropped from the scale through this procedure. Ensuing changes in the subscales from the original number of items to the final number of items ($n \rightarrow n$) were as follows:

Family subscale 19→12 items
Preferences subscale 24→11 items
Foods subscale 17→10 items
Attitudes subscale 33→7 items
Health subscale 36→12 items
Religion subscale 12→6 items
Childhood subscale 17→11 items
Superstitions subscale 31→5 items

The final set of items in the AAAS included the 74 items on which African Americans had scored significantly higher than all other ethnic groups and with which African Americans tended to agree. These 74 items measure eight, theoretically determined subscales. Reliability and validity of the total scale and of each of the subscales was then assessed.

Internal Consistency
and Split-Half Reliability

The 74 items were designed to assess the eight theoretical dimensions of African American culture detailed above, and so the items were grouped into eight subscales. The internal consistency reliability of these subscales was assessed for the sample as a whole. Those data are presented for each scale in Table 3.1, where the content of the 74 items also is shown. As indicated in Table 3.1, the eight subscales were highly reliable, with alphas ranging from .71 to .90. Reliability coefficients for the scales were as follows:

Family = .71
Preferences = .90
Foods = .81
Attitudes = .79
Health = .78
Religion = .76
Childhood = .81
Superstitions = .72

Thus, the items in each subscale measure the same underlying construct in a consistent, reliable manner. The split-half reliability of the 74 items was assessed by calculating the correlation between the average score on the 37 even-numbered items (Mean = 4.06, σ = 1.09) and the average score on the 37 odd-numbered items (Mean = 4.11, σ = 1.17). The resulting split-half reliability was r = .93, p = .0001. These internal consistency and split-half reliability data indicate that the AAAS is reliable.

Group Differences Validity

A multivariate analysis of variance (MANOVA) with follow-up analyses of variance (ANOVAs) was conducted to evaluate the extent to which African Americans differed from non-African Americans (treated as a whole) on the eight subscales; such group

(text continued on p. 74)

TABLE 3.1   Internal Consistency Reliability of African American Acculturation Scale Subscales

---

Subscale 1: Traditional Family Structures and Practices (Family; 12 items)

1. One or more of my relatives knows how to do hair.
2. When I was young, my parent(s) sent me to stay with a relative (aunt, uncle, grandmother) for a few days or weeks, and then I went back home again.
3. When I was young, I shared a bed at night with my sister, brother, or some other relative.
4. When I was young, my cousin, aunt, grandmother, or other relative lived with me and my family for a while.
5. When I was young, my mother or grandmother was the "real" head of the family.
6. When I was young, I took a bath with my sister, brother, or some other relative.
7. Old people are wise.
8. I often lend money or give other types of support to members of my family.
9. It's better to try to move your whole family ahead in this world than it is to be out for only yourself.
10. A child should not be allowed to call a grown woman by her first name, "Alice." The child should be taught to call her "Miss Alice."
11. It's best for infants to sleep with their mothers.
12. Some members of my family play the numbers.

                  Cronbach's Alpha   Standardized Item Alpha
                      .7077   .7147

Subscale 2: Preference for Things African American (Preferences; 11 items)

13. I know how to play bid whist.
14. Most of my friends are Black.
15. I feel more comfortable around Blacks than around Whites.
16. I listen to Black radio stations.
17. I try to watch all the Black shows on TV.
18. I read (or used to read) *Essence* or *Ebony* magazine.
19. Most of the music I listen to is by Black artists.
20. I like Black music more than White music.
21. The person I admire the most is Black.
22. When I pass a Black person (a stranger) on the street, I always say hello or nod at them.
23. I read (or used to read) *Jet* magazine.

                  Cronbach's Alpha   Standardized Item Alpha
                      .9020   .9001

Subscale 3: Preparation and Consumption of Traditional Foods (Foods; 10 items)

24. I usually add salt to my food to make it taste better.
25. I know how long you're supposed to cook collard greens.
26. I save grease from cooking to use it again later.
27. I know how to cook chit'lins.
28. I eat grits once in a while.
29. I eat a lot of fried food.

TABLE 3.1 Continued

30. Sometimes I eat collard greens.
31. Sometimes I cook ham hocks.
32. People say I eat too much salt.
33. I eat chit'lins once in a while.

    Cronbach's Alpha Standardized Item Alpha
     .8168   .8119

Subscale 4: Interracial Attitudes/Cultural Mistrust (Attitudes; 7 items)

34. Most tests (like the SATs and tests to get a job) are set up to make sure that Blacks don't get high scores on them.
35. Deep in their hearts, most White people are racists.
36. IQ tests were set up purposefully to discriminate against Black people.
37. Whites don't understand Blacks.
38. Some members of my family hate or distrust White people.
39. I don't trust most White people.
40. Most Whites are afraid of Blacks.

    Cronbach's Alpha Standardized Item Alpha
     .7870   .7877

Subscale 5: Traditional African American Health Beliefs and Practices (Health; 12 items)

41. There are many types of blood, such as "high," "low," "thin," and "bad" blood.
42. I was taught that you shouldn't take a bath and then go outside.
43. Illnesses can be classified as natural types and unnatural types.
44. I believe that some people know how to use voodoo.
45. Some people in my family use epsom salts.
46. I know what "falling out" means.
47. Some old Black women/ladies know how to cure diseases.
48. Some older Black women know a lot about pregnancy and childbirth.
49. Prayer can cure disease.
50. I have seen people "fall out."
51. If doctors can't cure you, you should try going to a root doctor or to your minister.
52. I have "fallen out."

    Cronbach's Alpha Standardized Item Alpha
     .7814   .7818

Subscale 6: Traditional African American Religious Beliefs and Practices (Religion; 6 items)

53. I believe in heaven and hell.
54. I like gospel music.
55. The church is the heart of the Black community.
56. I am currently a member of a Black church.
57. I have seen people "get the spirit" or speak in tongues.
58. I believe in the Holy Ghost.

    Cronbach's Alpha Standardized Item Alpha
     .7555   .7577

(continued)

TABLE 3.1 Continued

Subscale 7: Traditional African American Childhood Socialization (Childhood; 11 items)

59. I went to a mostly Black elementary school.
60. When I was young, I was a member of a Black church.
61. I grew up in a mostly Black neighborhood.
62. The biggest insult is an insult to your mother.
63. I went to (or go to) a mostly Black high school.
64. Dancing was an important part of my childhood.
65. I used to sing in the church choir.
66. When I was a child, I used to play tonk.
67. When I was young, I used to jump double-dutch.
68. I currently live in a mostly Black neighborhood.
69. I used to like to watch *Soul Train*.

	Cronbach's Alpha	Standardized Item Alpha
	.8118	.8106

Subscale 8: Superstitions (5 items)

70. What goes around, comes around.
71. There's some truth to many old superstitions.
72. I avoid splitting a pole.
73. When the palm of your hand itches, you'll receive some money.
74. I eat Black-eyed peas on New Year's Eve.

	Cronbach's Alpha	Standardized Item Alpha
	.7235	.7169

---

differences should be found in light of the procedure used to retain items. This MANOVA was significant, Hotelling's $T^2 = 2.24$; exact $F(8, 107) = 29.94, p = .0001$, indicating that African Americans differed from non-African Americans on the linear composite of the eight subscales. The ANOVAs from this analysis are presented in Table 3.2. As indicated by the group means and ANOVAs in Table 3.2, African Americans scored higher than non-African Americans on each of the eight subscales. The scores on these eight subscales were then added to yield a total score on the AAAS. A t-test was then calculated and indicated that the mean total AAAS score for African Americans (343.01) was higher than for non-African Americans (201.55); this average difference of 141.47 points was highly significant ($t = 13.03$, $p = .0001$).

TABLE 3.2   Group-Differences Validity of the African American
Acculturation Scale: African Americans Versus Other
Ethnic Groups Combined

Subscale	African Americans	All Other Ethnic Groups	SS	F^{ab}
Traditional Family				
Structures and Practices	56.51	41.61	6009.44	41.19
Preference for Things				
African American	53.02	21.47	26945.21	149.64
Preparation and Consumption				
of Traditional Foods	43.95	23.67	11119.23	87.95
Interracial Attitudes/				
Cultural Mistrust	28.86	18.06	3159.17	39.81
Traditional African American				
Health Beliefs and Practices	52.27	36.05	7125.81	38.96
Traditional African American				
Religious Beliefs and Practices	35.25	22.30	4534.06	92.59
Traditional African American				
Childhood Socialization	52.97	25.79	19993.69	174.40
Superstitions	20.19	12.61	1554.91	34.79
Total AAAS	343.01	201.55		$t = 13.03$

a. df 1, 114 for each F
b. All differences are significant at the $p = .0001$ level.

Relationships Among Subscales

Because the various aspects of a culture are related to each
other, correlations among the subscales of the AAAS should be
found. These correlations (based on the African Americans only)
are shown in Table 3.3, along with significance tests for each r
and the correlations between each subscale and the total AAAS
score. As indicated in Table 3.3, many significant correlations
among the subscales were found and were theoretically sensible,
with all subscales having moderate to strong correlations with
the total scale score. The Family subscale correlated highest (.82)
with the total AAAS score, followed by the Health (.78) and
Childhood (.72) scales.

TABLE 3.3 Correlations Among Subscales

	Traditional Family Structures and Practices	Preferences	Foods	Interracial Attitudes	Health	Religion	Childhood	Superstition
Preference for Things Black	.42***							
Food	.51***	.23*						
Interracial Attitudes	.32*	.39***	.02[a]					
Health	.64***	.34**	.42***	.35***				
Religion	.27*	.23*	.28**	.12[a]	.31**			
Socialization	.47*	.53***	.44***	.26*	.39***	.29**		
Superstition	.49***	.29**	.49***	.41***	.50***	.08[a]	.28**	
AAAS Total	.82***	.67***	.66***	.49***	.78***	.40***	.72***	.61***

a. not significant.
*$p = .02$; **$p = .005$; ***$p = .0001$.

Concurrent Validity

Theoretically, members of any ethnic group who live in an ethnic-minority enclave are likely to be the more traditional members of their culture, if only because of constant exposure to the culture; likewise, those who live in predominately European American or integrated neighborhoods are likely to be more acculturated. If the AAAS scale measures acculturation, then African Americans who live in African American enclaves should score higher than those who live elsewhere; such a finding would provide preliminary evidence for the concurrent validity of the scale. To assess this, we examined scores on the question "I currently live in a Black neighborhood" (a question on the Childhood subscale), and divided the African American participants into two groups: The *other residence group* were the 31 African Americans who circled 1 = *this is not at all true of me* and the *African American enclave group* were the 41 African Americans who circled 7 = *this is absolutely true of me.* We ran a multivariate analysis of variance to assess the extent to which these two groups differed on the eight subscales; the criterion item above, used to define groups, was removed from the Childhood subscale for this analysis. This MANOVA was significant, Hotelling's T^2 = .568, Exact $F(8, 42)$ = 2.98, p = .01, indicating that African Americans who live in African American enclaves differed from those living elsewhere on the subscales. Follow-up, one-way ANOVAs were then conducted and are presented in Table 3.4.

As indicated in Table 3.4, African Americans who live in African American enclaves scored significantly higher than those living elsewhere on these four of the eight subscales: Family, Preferences, Foods, and Attitudes. Differences on the remaining four subscales, although not statistically significant, were all in the predicted direction (i.e., those who lived in African American enclaves had higher scores) and might have reached significance with larger samples.

Finally, a *t*-test to assess the extent to which the African American enclave and other-residence subjects differed on the Total

TABLE 3.4 Concurrent Validity of the AAAS Subscales and Total Score

AAAS Subscale	Means for Subjects Who Live in Enclaves (n = 31)	Means for Subjects Who Live Elsewhere (n = 41)	Sum of Squares	F
Family	61.29	51.21	1293.04	7.51***
Preference for Things Black	59.85	49.46	1372.56	8.67***
Food	48.26	39.08	1069.81	6.21*
Interracial Attitudes	31.59	25.58	458.83	5.34*
Health	55.89	48.58	678.13	2.95[a]
Religion	34.89	34.58	1.19	0.02[a]
Socialization	51.41	46.38	321.78	2.63[a]
Superstition	21.07	19.17	46.23	0.69[a]
Total AAAS score	364.26	314.04		$t = -3.10$**

a. not significant.

*$p < .02$; **$p = .003$; ***$p < .005$.

AAAS scale also was computed, with the prediction that the former would score higher than the latter. The mean Total AAAS score for African Americans from ethnic enclaves was 364.26, and for African Americans who live elsewhere, 314.04. This difference of 50.22 points in their scores was highly significant, $t(49) = -3.10$, $p < .003$. Thus, African Americans who live in African American enclaves scored higher than those who live elsewhere on four of the eight subscales and on the total AAAS score; these data provide initial evidence for the concurrent validity of the scale.

Further Validity Checks: Status Variables

The AAAS is intended to measure acculturation, that is, the extent to which individuals are immersed in African American culture. Acculturation should not be related to education, social class, or other status variables, particularly given the principle of return described in Chapter 2. Thus, if this scale measures aspects of African American culture rather than aspects of status, no significant relationships between scores on the scale and status variables should be found; this would provide additional evidence for the validity of the scale and answer the question of whether we are measuring African American culture or the beliefs of poor and uneducated African Americans. To evaluate this issue, we ran a series of MANOVAs (for the African American subjects only) to assess the extent to which scores on the eight subscales were related to city of origin, education, income, and gender.

The MANOVA across the subscales by city of origin (e.g., the subject grew up in an urban versus suburban or rural environment) was not significant, Hotelling's $T^2 = .073$, $F(8, 69) = 0.63$; subjects who grew up in large cities $(n = 73)$ did not score differently from those who grew up in suburbs or in rural areas $(n = 44)$ on any of the subscales (all follow-up ANOVAs were not significant). The MANOVA by education level also was not significant, Hotelling's $T^2 = .368$, $F(24, 97) = 1.01$, and none of the follow-up ANOVAs was significant; scores were similar

whether the subject had less than a high school education (n = 25),
was a high school graduate (n = 20), had some college (n = 47),
or had graduated from college and/or graduate school (n = 31).
Likewise, the MANOVA by current income was not significant,
T^2 = 6.06, $F(24, 146)$ = 1.29, and none of the one-way ANOVAs
was significant; no differences in scores were found whether
subjects were poor (0-$13,200 per year, n = 35), had lower-middle-
class incomes ($15,000-$28,400 per year, n = 30), or had middle-
and upper-middle-class incomes ($31,000-$80,000 per year, n =
17). The MANOVA for gender similarly was not significant,
T^2 = .127, $F(8, 69)$ = 1.09; men and women did not differ in
their scores.

These data suggest that the AAAS does not measure social
class or education but rather maintenance of aspects of African
American culture that transcend these status characteristics.

Scores of African Americans

The scores of African Americans, both total scores and subscale
scores, differed widely (e.g., a range of more than 200 points on
the total AAAS score). Some African Americans scored extremely
low (acculturated), and others scored extremely high (traditional),
as shown by the means, medians, and modes in Table 3.5. As
indicated above, these differences cannot be attributed to the
social class, gender, or education of the subjects, and so they
must represent differences in levels of acculturation. Likewise,
this variance suggests that there was no response bias (e.g., a
tendency to strongly agree with items about African American
culture simply because they are about African American culture),
for many subjects strongly disagreed with the items. Thus again,
these differences may accurately represent differences in African
American levels of acculturation.

DISCUSSION OF STUDY 1

These analyses suggest that the AAAS has good internal
consistency and split-half reliability, as well as group differences

TABLE 3.5 Variance in African American Scores and Comparison to Non-African Americans

Scale		Range of Scores	Mean	Standard Deviation	Median	Mode
Family	Blacks	27-81	56.51	12.57	57	54
	All others	18-77	41.61	11.51	43	57
Preference for Things Black	Blacks	18-75	53.02	13.03	56	57
	All others	11-60	21.47	12.26	20.50	11
Food	Blacks	13-69	43.95	12.94	45	43
	All others	10-52	23.67	10.87	24.5	22
Interracial Attitudes	Blacks	7-45	28.86	9.04	28.50	22
	All others	7-42	18.06	7.87	18	18
Health	Blacks	18-84	52.27	13.93	53	57
	All others	14-66	36.05	11.83	34	28
Religion	Blacks	13-42	35.25	7.29	36	42
	All others	6-41	22.30	7.87	23	17
Socialization	Blacks	23-75	52.97	11.14	52	53
	All others	11-62	25.79	11.58	25	21
Superstition	Blacks	5-35	20.19	7.73	22	23
	All others	5-25	12.61	4.69	12	11
AAAS Total	Blacks	201-463	343.01	60.76	340.50	306
	All others	104-317	201.55	48.89	196	169

and concurrent validity. In addition, the scale was normed on a community sample (rather than on college students) of African American adults of a diversity of ages, social classes, and education levels and from a variety of geographical regions. The diversity of the sample matches the diversity of the African American community, suggesting that the scale may have broad utility. The diversity of the sample also suggests that the scale can be read and understood by people with limited education (i.e., one fifth of our sample had not finished high school). Thus, although this sample was quite small and cross-validation with another is needed, our preliminary evidence suggests that the AAAS has sufficient validity and reliability to be used by researchers. The scale is presented in Appendix B at the end of this book for that purpose, and we extend permission to others to use it.

We developed this scale with the hope of encouraging research on the relationship between African American acculturation and a variety of psychological variables. More specifically, our hope was that, by using our scale, other researchers might demonstrate that the psychological and behavioral differences between African Americans and other groups can be understood as a manifestation of cultural context (operationalized as acculturation). Such research has the potential to reduce racist interpretations of the differences between African Americans and European Americans by shedding a clear cultural light on behavior. Likewise, future research using our scale also has the potential to reduce the racist perception of African Americans as a homogenous group through studies demonstrating considerable variability in levels of acculturation, and so in the beliefs, practices, and behaviors entailed therein. Thus, we strongly encourage research with this scale in all areas of psychology. In addition, we hope that research using this scale might lead to a deeper appreciation of African Americans as a cultural (ethnic) group who share some cultural traditions (co-sleeping, a belief in the power of prayer) with other ethnic minorities in America and deserve to be regarded similarly; we hope that the use of this scale can reduce the tendency to regard African Americans as a race, as discussed at length in Chapter 1.

The tendency to regard African Americans solely or primarily as a racial rather than an ethnic group has meant that aspects of African American culture that may have important psychological implications (e.g., the sequelae of co-sleeping and informal adoption) remain unexplored.

As we found here, many aspects of African American culture (some of which predate slavery) clearly persist among African Americans, regardless of social class and education. Our participants who live on welfare in the most dilapidated section of South Central Los Angeles scored in a manner similar to our educated, upper-middle-class ($80,000 per year) subjects "living large" in the wealthy suburbs nearby. Although preliminary, then, nonetheless these data provide yet another type of evidence for the existence of a common African American culture that transcends the large social class and education differences among that population. Such findings are incompatible with the popular view (put forth by Wilson, 1980) that the differences between European Americans and African Americans are solely an issue of social class and that the social class differences among African Americans themselves are so large that no common culture could survive or transcend them. Our data are thereby encouraging.

Finally, questions regarding the relationship between African American acculturation and Black racial identity need to be addressed, because the latter construct has received considerable empirical attention. This issue is addressed briefly below.

Black racial identity, measured by the Racial Identity Attitude Scale (RIAS, see Helms, 1990, for a comprehensive review of the theory and the major studies), refers to the extent to which people identify with the racial group to which they belong. Specifically, it "refers to the quality or manner of one's identification with the respective racial group" (Helms, 1990, p. 5). Racial identity as such can be conceptualized along a continuum (reflected in a diversity of competing identity stage theories) from denial of membership in one's group and racist beliefs about one's own race, on the one hand, to acceptance of and pride in one's racial group membership on the other.

Racial identity so defined is independent of the construct of acculturation. That is, traditional African Americans (living in an African American neighborhood, eating traditional foods, and belonging to a traditional church) may have a racial identity at either end of that continuum, as well as anywhere along it. They may hold racist beliefs about African Americans and hate their racial group membership or accept and take pride in that membership, depending on the attitudes and behavior of their parents, kin, teachers, coworkers, and community, as well as on the behavior of European Americans toward them. Likewise, highly acculturated African Americans (e.g., who have adopted some aspects of the dominant culture in order to succeed in some specific dominant local environment) may accept and take pride in their race or may reject and deny their racial group membership. Theoretically, then, acculturation and racial identity are orthogonal constructs. Scores on the majority of the AAAS subscales should not be related to scores on the RIAS. However, we do strongly suspect that scores on the Preferences subscale of the AAAS will be related to racial identity, because this subscale is in some ways similar to the racial identity construct.

Finally, a careful examination of our items similarly reveals that scores on most of the AAAS subscales are probably unrelated to racial identity. For example, the fact that one might agree with the following items reveals nothing whatsoever about one's attitudes toward and identification with one's race (racial identity):

I believe in the Holy Ghost.
Prayer can cure disease.
As a child I used to play tonk.

Rather, these items reveal the extent of one's participation in the beliefs and practices of one's culture (acculturation). Inevitably, however, the relationship between these constructs is an empirical question necessitating an empirical answer. We encourage such research.

STUDY 2

The second study was a cross-validation study involving a new sample of African American adults (Sample 2). The objectives of this study were to (a) assess the reliability of the scale with a new sample, and (b) assess the relationship between the scores of the new and the original samples.

PARTICIPANTS AND PROCEDURE

A questionnaire consisting of the AAAS and demographic questions was completed by 175 African American adults (67 men, 108 women). The participants' ages ranged from 17 to 59 years (Mean = 26, σ = 9), and their average level of education was 13 years.

These African Americans were approached in one community organization (n = 17), one African American church (n = 44), one 4-year college (n = 48), and one 2-year community (junior) college (n = 66) and asked to complete an anonymous survey on African American attitudes and beliefs. Thus, although the previous sample consisted of 123 African American adults (Mean age = 32.8 years) sampled in community organizations, the current sample consisted of younger (Mean age = 26) adults who were primarily college students (114 of the 175 African American subjects, or 65%, were college students).

STUDY 2 RESULTS

The scores of the previous sample (African Americans from Study 1) were compared to those of the current sample by conducting a multivariate analysis of variance (MANOVA) with standard, follow-up ANOVAs. These data are shown in Table 3.6. The MANOVA was significant, Hotelling's T^2 = .2609, Exact $F(8,292)$ = 9.52, p = .0005, indicating that the two samples differed in their scores on the AAAS. The ANOVAs shown in Table 3.6 revealed that Sample 1 scored higher than the current

TABLE 3.6 ANOVAs Comparing Scores of African Americans From Two Samples

Scale	Range Possible	Sample	Obtained Range	σ	Mode	Median	Mean	Sum of Squares	F[a]
Family	12-84	Study 1	27-81	12.57	54	57.00	56.51	565.96	3.46
		Study 2	25-82	12.59	39	53.00	53.12		
Preference for Things Black	7-77	Study 1	18-75	13.03	57	56.00	53.02	175.550	.97
		Study 2	13-76	13.72	62	59.00	54.51		
Food	10-70	Study 1	13-69	12.94	43	45.00	43.95	5425.21	28.56**
		Study 2	11-69	13.61	31	34.00	36.14		
Interracial Attitudes	7-49	Study 1	7-45	7.87	18	18.00	28.86	363.89	4.19*
		Study 2	7-49	9.38	25	31.00	30.29		
Health	12-84	Study 1	18-84	13.93	57	53.00	52.27	194.02	1.00
		Study 2	15-84	14.17	42	55.20	53.52		
Religion	6-42	Study 1	13-42	7.29	42	36.00	35.25	236.12	2.95
		Study 2	6-42	9.43	42	33.00	31.54		
Socialization	11-77	Study 1	23-75	11.14	53	52.00	52.97	4148.52	28.27**
		Study 2	17-77	12.83	47	45.00	44.53		
Superstitions	5-35	Study 1	5-35	7.73	23	22.00	20.19	5.66	0.86
		Study 2	5-35	7.15	14	19.00	20.32		
AAAS Total	74-518	Study 1	201-463	60.76	306	340.50	343.01	$t(299) = -2.25$[b]	
		Study 2	143-512	61.69	323	323.00	318.67		

a. $df = 1,299$ for each F.
b. This t-test ($df = 299$) on the total score was conducted separately, $p = .03$.
*$p = .05$; **$p = .005$.

TABLE 3.7 Internal Consistency Reliability (Cronbach's Alpha)
of Subscales With Two Samples

Subscale	Study 1	Study 2
Family	.71	.64
Preference for Things Black	.90	.83
Food	.81	.79
Interracial Attitudes	.79	.83
Health	.78	.78
Religious	.76	.81
Socialization	.81	.69
Superstition	.72	.67

one on two subscales (Foods and Childhood) and, consequently, on the total AAAS score, whereas Sample 2 scored higher on the Attitudes subscale. These two samples differed significantly in terms of age—the current sample is significantly younger than the former one: $t(285) = -5.62, p = .0005$—and residence: Sample 2 lives in White/integrated and Sample 1 in African American neighborhoods, $\chi^2 (1) = 17.36, p = .00003$. Nevertheless, they differed on only three of the eight subscales (37.5%), with no differences on the majority of the subscales. These data suggest that young college student samples and older community samples obtain similar scores on the AAAS.

We next assessed the extent to which the reliability of the subscales was similar for the two samples. In Table 3.7, the internal consistency reliability of the subscales with Sample 2 is displayed and compared to the reliabilities found with Sample 1. As indicated, the reliabilities were highly similar. Using the Fisher r to z transformation (Hays, 1981), we tested these reliability coefficients for significant differences. No differences between the reliabilities for the two samples were found.

These data suggest that college student samples and community samples score similarly on the AAAS and that the subscales remain reliable across these kinds of samples; the data thereby constitute initial cross-validation of the scale. We can now turn to an analysis of the relationship between levels of acculturation among African Americans and behavior.

4

Acculturation and Physical Health

In this chapter, we examine the relationship between levels of acculturation and health behavior/health status among African American adults. Specifically, we examine acculturation and cigarette smoking (one important health behavior) and acculturation and high blood pressure (one important aspect of health status). In Chapter 5, we will examine the relationship between levels of acculturation and mental health among African Americans.

STUDY 3: CIGARETTE SMOKING

Smoking is an important behavior to study because it remains the single most preventable cause of death (U.S. Department of Health, Education, and Welfare, 1979), accounting for 30% of all deaths from cancer each year (125,000 people per year; American

Cancer Society, 1989). Smoking also plays a major, causative role in heart disease, stroke, and hypertension, accounting for an additional 170,000 deaths annually from cardiovascular disease (Centers for Disease Control, 1989). These smoking-related health problems (i.e., cancer, stroke, hypertension, and cardiovascular disease) are foremost among the major health problems of the African American community, are more prevalent among African Americans than among Whites (Hildreth & Saunders, 1992; Polednak, 1989), and are prevalent among African American women in particular (Klonoff, Landrine, & Scott, 1995). In addition, smoking among pregnant women results in infants with low birth weights, an additional health problem in the African American community (Centers for Disease Control, 1989). Finally, smoking acts as a "gateway drug" and plays a major role in later substance abuse; youth who smoke cigarettes are more likely than those who do not to later abuse alcohol, marijuana, and other drugs (e.g., Fleming, Leventhal, Glynn, & Ershler, 1989). Thus understanding the variables involved in cigarette smoking among African Americans is extremely important because such data can lead to more effective, culturally tailored smoking prevention and cessation programs; these programs, in turn, can reduce deaths from cardiovascular disease, stroke, and cancer; reduce hypertension; reduce and prevent the childhood behavioral problems and neuropsychological deficits that are secondary to low birth weight; and reduce drug abuse among African American youth as well.

It is widely acknowledged that acculturation plays a role in cigarette smoking among Latino children (e.g., Landrine, Richardson, et al., 1994; Marín, Marín, Otero-Sabogal, Sabogal, & Perez-Stable, 1989), young adults (Smith, McGraw, & Carrillo, 1991), and adults (Marín, Perez-Stable, & Marín, 1989; Markides, Coreil, & Ray, 1987), and thus cultural variables are addressed in smoking prevention and cessation programs for Latinos (e.g., Botvin & Eng, 1980). The role of acculturation in smoking among African Americans has not been addressed, however, perhaps because of the absence (until recently) of our scale, which assesses levels of acculturation among African Americans and thereby permits examination of the role of African American acculturation in health-related behaviors. The purpose of this study was to begin to examine the role of African American acculturation in cigarette smoking among adults, with the hope that such data may shed light on how to tailor smoking prevention and cessation programs for the African American population.

We began with the hypothesis that acculturation plays a significant role in smoking among African Americans and that the relationship between acculturation and cigarette smoking among African American adults might be similar to that found for Latino adults. Thus, consistent with the findings of Marín, Perez-Stable, et al. (1989) for Latinos, we hypothesized that smokers would tend to be traditional (less acculturated) and nonsmokers more acculturated.

PARTICIPANTS, MATERIALS, AND PROCEDURE

The 118 African American adults who participated in the first study to develop the AAAS (Sample 1, Chapter 3) were the participants in this study; 10 additional African Americans from that sample, whose questionnaires were not available at the time of Study 1, are included here. Thus, there were 128 African American adults (50 men, 78 women) who ranged in age from 15 to 70 years (Mean = 33.5, σ = 11.4 years), and their incomes from zero to $80,000 annually (Mean = $17,622, σ = 17,222). The procedures for obtaining data from this sample were detailed in Chapter 3.

The sample completed an anonymous questionnaire consisting of the AAAS, demographic questions, and the question "Do you smoke?" to be answered yes or no.

RESULTS

Subjects were divided into Smokers (n = 59) and Nonsmokers (n = 69). A multivariate analysis of variance (MANOVA), with the eight subscales of the AAAS as dependent variables, was conducted to assess the extent to which these groups differed in level of acculturation. This MANOVA was significant, Hotelling's T^2 = .185, Exact $F(8, 119)$ = 2.75, p = .008, indicating that smokers and nonsmokers differed on the acculturation subscales. Followup ANOVAs are shown in Table 4.1.

As indicated in Table 4.1, smokers scored higher (more traditional, less acculturated) than nonsmokers on four of the eight subscales (Preparation and Consumption of Traditional Foods, Interracial Attitudes/Cultural Mistrust, Traditional African American Health Beliefs and Practices, Superstitions). Smokers had more traditional health beliefs, more strongly endorsed cultural superstitions, had more traditional interracial attitudes (greater distrust of Whites), and were more likely than nonsmokers to prepare and consume traditional foods. Smokers (Mean = 354.04) also scored higher than nonsmokers (Mean = 329.14) on the AAAS total score, $t(124)$ = 2.40, p < .02, indicating a more traditional cultural orientation.

To assure that the differences between smokers and nonsmokers reflect acculturation rather than social class, a t-test comparing their incomes was calculated. The result, $t(94)$ = −1.15, p = .26) was not significant, indicating that smokers (Mean Annual Income = $15,661, σ = $16,911) and nonsmokers (Mean Annual Income = $19,671, σ = $17,364) did not differ in social class. To assure that these findings reflect acculturation rather than neighborhood, a chi-square was computed and compared the neighborhoods in which smokers and nonsmokers lived. If smokers tend to live in ethnically homogenous, African American enclaves or neighborhoods (as opposed to integrated or White neighborhoods), then (a) their smoking may reflect the tobacco industry's advertising campaign (to increase the number of smokers) in African American neighborhoods (Davis, 1987) and (b) they may have scored as more traditional on the AAAS simply because their neighborhoods assure that they are frequently exposed to African American culture. Smokers' high (traditional) scores on the AAAS and their smoking may both be an artifact of residence. This chi-square (Smoker v. Nonsmoker

TABLE 4.1 Differences Between Smokers and Nonsmokers on the AAAS

	Smokers	Nonsmokers	SS	F^a	p
Family	57.85	54.19	417.87	2.57	ns
Preference for Things Black	53.09	52.97	0.47	0.00	ns
Food	47.82	42.52	882.88	5.52	.02
Interracial Attitudes	30.05	26.53	387.33	4.87	.03
Health	55.13	49.42	1023.93	6.14	.02
Religion	33.02	34.05	33.41	0.53	ns
Socialization	53.72	50.65	295.59	2.34	ns
Superstition	23.35	18.79	652.39	12.83	.0005

NOTE: ns = not significant.
a. $df = 1, 124$ for each F above.

by Black v. Other Neighborhood) was not significant, however
(χ^2 [1] = .89, p = .34). Smokers were more traditional and
Nonsmokers more acculturated, and these differences were not
an artifact of social class or type of neighborhood.

DISCUSSION

These data suggest that African American smokers tend to be
more traditional than their nonsmoking counterparts. Smokers
had greater distrust of Whites, more traditional (non-Western)
health beliefs, endorsed more superstitions, and were more likely
to eat traditional foods than Nonsmokers. These data may mean
that traditional African Americans distrust Whites to such an
extent that they distrust information about smoking provided by
Whites. Indeed, the relationship between the Attitudes, Superstitions, Health, and Foods subscales on which smokers scored
high may be a causal one, in which distrust of Whites (Attitudes
subscale) leads to distrust of health information provided by Whites
(Health subscale)—including information on the dangers of con-
suming heavily salted, fried food (Foods subscale) and of smoking.
Alternatively, these findings may mean that highly traditional
African Americans are precisely that: members of the culture
who retain the unhealthy lifestyle that has fallen out of fashion
in the larger, European American culture simply because they are
detached from it. Likewise, given that smokers and nonsmokers
differed on the Superstitions and Health subscales, it also is
possible that African American smokers believe that they render
themselves invulnerable to the deleterious consequences of
smoking by engaging in traditional health practices and various
superstitious rituals. This latter possibility is consistent with the
finding that African American smokers exhibit little concern
about the health consequences of smoking relative to their European American, Asian, and Hispanic counterparts; they seem to
believe that they will suffer few health consequences (Martin,
Cummings, & Coates, 1990).

In either case, these data suggest that smoking prevention and cessation programs may need to target traditional African Americans (the likely smokers) and be conducted by African Americans (in light of smokers' high distrust of Whites). In addition, such programs may need to be culturally tailored and offered through the settings that traditional African Americans frequent (e.g., churches) to reach the smokers in this culture. Although there appears to be at least one smoking-cessation program conducted through African American churches (Stillman, Bone, & Rand, 1993), there appear to be no smoking-prevention programs conducted in such settings. Health promotion and disease prevention programs have neglected traditional African Americans and must devote increased attention to their health.

An Alternative Hypothesis

One final possible explanation for these findings must be considered. This is the possibility that traditional African Americans experience significantly greater emotional distress (depression, anxiety, tension) than their more acculturated counterparts because the two groups are treated differently by European Americans. For example, to European Americans, traditional African Americans may seem to be more prototypically or stereotypically "Black" than their acculturated counterparts, and thus they may experience greater racial discrimination. This in turn could result in higher levels of stress, depression, and anxiety, and those negative affective states could then lead to greater smoking. We considered this possibility to be more compelling than the other possible explanations offered above because some empirical evidence supports this interpretation. For example, one study (Gottlieb & Green, 1987) found that high stress was related to smoking among African American adults. Likewise, although the role of depression and anxiety in smoking among African American adults has not been investigated, studies have found these negative affective states to be strongly associated with smoking among

European American adults (e.g., Breslau, Kilbey, & Andreski, 1991). In addition, it seems reasonable to suspect that the more traditional members of any ethnic minority group face more discrimination than their acculturated counterparts. For example, Latinos and Asians who speak with thick accents (traditional) may be viewed as more "foreign" than their acculturated counterparts, who speak without such accents (because English is their first, not second language), and they may experience greater discrimination. Our hypothesis for African Americans may hold for other groups as well. Thus, we examine this hypothesis later in this chapter. We turn now to an exploration of the role of acculturation in hypertension among African Americans.

STUDY 4: SELF-REPORTED
HIGH BLOOD PRESSURE

Although hypertension is one of the most serious health problems among African Americans (Hildreth & Saunders, 1992; Polednak, 1989), no studies have addressed the relationship between hypertension and acculturation for this population. We explored that relationship with a new, independent sample (Sample 3) of 153 African Americans.

PARTICIPANTS AND PROCEDURE

Sample 3 consisted of 153 African Americans (83 women, 66 men, 4 unidentified) whose ages ranged from 15 to 70 (Mean = 30.14 years, $\sigma = 11.66$ years). The majority ($n = 85$ or 57.8%) were single, 40 (27.2 %) were married, and the remainder were separated, widowed, or divorced. Thirty-four (22.8 %) were high school graduates, 66 (44.3%) were college students, 38 (25.5%) had college degrees, and 11 (7.4%) had master's or doctorate degrees. Their annual incomes ranged from zero to $80,000 (Mean = $21,451, $\sigma = $17,175). They were approached on college campuses and in the community (organizations, clubs) and asked to complete an anonymous questionnaire.

MATERIALS

The questionnaire consisted of several instruments, some of which are not relevant to this discussion and will be addressed in a later chapter. Instruments and items included that are relevant to this discussion are the AAAS and demographic questions. An additional item asked "Has your doctor told you that you have high blood pressure?" to be answered yes or no. Although measured blood pressure is the more desirable assessment procedure, studies (e.g., Krieger, 1990) have shown that self-reports of high blood pressure, *when requested in this manner,* match measured blood pressure. Analyses are based on the 142 of the 153 subjects who answered the blood pressure question.

RESULTS AND DISCUSSION

Subjects were divided into two groups; the hypertension group was the 22 subjects who reported high blood pressure, and the normotensive group was the 115 who reported normal blood pressure; 5 subjects who did not complete the entire AAAS were omitted from the analyses. A MANOVA (using the eight subscales of the AAAS as dependent variables) was conducted and was significant, Hotelling's $T^2 = 0.15$, Exact $F(8, 124) = 2.30$, $p = .025$, indicating that the two blood pressure groups differed on the AAAS. Follow-up ANOVAs are shown in Table 4.2.

As shown in Table 4.2, the hypertensives scored higher (more traditional) than the normotensives on two AAAS subscales (Traditional African American Childhood Socialization and Foods) and consequently on the total AAAS score (t-test shown in Table 4.2). Hypertensives tended to be more traditional and normotensives more acculturated.

There are two possible interpretations of these findings. One possibility is that traditional African Americans have higher

TABLE 4.2 Hypertensive and Normotensive Group Differences on the AAAS Subscales

AAAS Scale	Normotensive Group Mean	Hypertensive Group Mean	SS	F[a]	p
Family	48.45	51.99	230.01	1.37	ns
Preference for Things Black	52.21	52.57	2.40	0.02	ns
Food	32.18	41.69	1661.15	8.74	.004
Interracial Attitudes	27.59	31.68	308.08	3.29	ns
Health	49.17	53.57	355.07	1.32	ns
Religion	31.80	34.23	108.18	1.25	ns
Socialization	42.92	50.73	1118.18	6.30	.013
Superstition	18.25	19.36	22.68	0.41	ns
Total AAAS Scale	302.57	335.82	$t(131) = -2.27$[b]		.025

NOTE: ns = not significant.
a. $df = (1, 131)$ for each F above.
b. This t-test on the total score was conducted separately.

blood pressure than their more acculturated counterparts because they consume traditional, cultural foods more frequently (differences on the Foods subscale). These foods (e.g., collard greens, chitterlings, fried chicken) tend to be high in salt content, and salt intake is a major variable in hypertension among African Americans (Hildreth & Saunders, 1992; Polednak, 1989). If consumption of traditional foods accounts for the relationship between acculturation and hypertension, then hypertensive African Americans may benefit from counseling and advice from registered dietitians who are sensitive to cultural food preferences (Hildreth & Saunders, 1992). Likewise, efforts to prevent hypertension among African Americans may need to address alternative (low-salt) procedures for preparing traditional foods, so that consumption of these can be maintained in a healthy manner.

Alternatively, as hypothesized for smoking, traditional African Americans may have higher blood pressure than their acculturated counterparts because they experience more frequent racial discrimination. Differences found between hypertensives and normotensives on the Childhood subscale may mean that more traditionally socialized African Americans seem "more Black" and are treated badly by European Americans. Support for this latter hypothesis was provided by Krieger (1990), who found a strong relationship between reports of racial discrimination and high blood pressure among African Americans. Additional support comes from studies that have found strong relationships among anger, rage, and hypertension (e.g., James, 1987; Sommers-Flanagan & Greenberg, 1989). Although these studies have not addressed racism as the reason and cause for anger and rage among African Americans, other studies indicate clearly that racism is the life event about which African Americans are most angry (Cose, 1993; Jones, 1986). Indeed, pent-up rage about racism is the single most common problem presented by African Americans who seek psychotherapy (National Institute of Mental Health, 1983). Thus level of acculturation may predict amount of racial discrimination, and amount of racial discrimination may predict both cigarette smoking and hypertension. We address these hypotheses below.

RACISM, ACCULTURATION,
AND PHYSICAL HEALTH

In the previous studies, we found that smokers and hypertensives tended to be more traditional than their nonsmoking and normotensive counterparts, respectively. We hypothesized that this is because more traditional African Americans are perceived as "more Black" than their acculturated cohorts; that they consequently experience greater racial discrimination (a culturally specific stressor); and that this racism then results in increased stress, anger, cigarette smoking, and blood pressure. This hypothesis is reasonable in light of data indicating that discrimination against African Americans is rampant. For example, studies have found that African Americans are discriminated against in a variety of arenas, ranging from face-to-face interactions (Landrine, Klonoff, Alcaraz, Scott, & Wilkins, 1995), to discrimination in housing, employment, health, and social services (Feagin & Feagin, 1978; Idson & Price, 1992; Krieger, 1990). African Americans (middle-class, successful ones in particular) report experiencing racial discrimination (or *racist events*) so frequently (Cose, 1993; Jones, 1986; Jones & Korchin, 1982) that depression, tension, and rage about racism is the single most common problem presented by African Americans in psychotherapy (National Institute of Mental Health, 1983). Such discrimination undoubtedly has negative physical and mental health consequences (NIMH, 1983) that are widely recognized (Chunn, Dunston, & Ross-Sheriff, 1983; Jones & Korchin, 1982). Nonetheless, the role of racism in physical and mental health among African Americans rarely has been addressed empirically.

We suspect that the reason for the paucity of studies on the sequela of racism is the absence of a scale that assesses and quantifies racial discrimination, so that its role in African American physical and mental health can be examined. We recently created such a scale, *The Schedule of Racist Events* (Landrine & Klonoff, 1996) and discuss it only briefly here. This is because the purpose of this chapter is not to fully examine the role of racism in African American physical and mental health but, rather, to test the hypothesis that racism accounts for the relationship between hypertension, smoking, and acculturation found and reported here. Thus, the many validity and reliability studies conducted on our racism scale are not addressed here.

RACIST EVENTS AS
CULTURALLY SPECIFIC STRESSORS

Racial discrimination takes a variety of forms and includes being called racist names such as "nigger"; being discriminated against by people in various professions; being discriminated against by strangers; being accused or suspected of wrongdoing (stealing, cheating); being discriminated against by institutions, such as banks and schools in applications for loans, scholarships, admission, and the like. These various types of racial discrimination can all be conceptualized as specific racist events, which are analogous to the generic (can happen to anyone) life events (e.g., getting fired) and generic hassles (e.g., losing your car keys) assessed by popular measures of stressful events (e.g., the PERI-Life Events Scale; Dohrenwend, Krasnoff, Askenasy, & Dohrenwend, 1978; and the Hassles Frequency scale; Kanner, Coyne, Schaeffer, & Lazarus, 1981). Thus, we conceptualize the various domains/types of racial discrimination as racist events and view racist events as culturally specific, negative life events, that is, as culturally specific stressors. Racist events can be viewed as culturally specific stressors because they are negative events (stressors) that happen to African Americans, because they are African Americans.

By conceptualizing racist events (racial discrimination) as culturally specific, negative life events or stressors that are analogous to generic life events, theoretical models and lines of investigation from stress research (e.g., Lazarus, 1966; Lazarus,

DeLongis, Folkman, & Gruen, 1985; Lazarus & Launier, 1978) can be applied. Thus racist events can be conceptualized as occurring frequently or infrequently and so might be measured in that manner. Like other stressful life events, racist events also can be conceptualized as acute (recent) and chronic (lifetime), and the impact of recent versus lifetime racial discrimination on physical and mental health can be examined. This approach focuses on the *frequency* with which African Americans have experienced specific racist events recently, as well as throughout their entire lives.

There are, however, two global, significantly different approaches to measuring stress. One approach focuses on the frequency with which people experience specific events that are known or presumed to be stressful. This events approach uses scales such as the Hassles Frequency Scale and the PERI-LES. The frequency of stressful events is summed and used as a measure of stress. This is only one way that we could measure racist events, however. The alternative approach focuses on the *appraisal* (evaluation) of events and situations as stressful and uses scales such as the Perceived Stress Scale (Cohen, Kamarck, & Mermelstein, 1983). The logic behind the appraisal approach is that two people may experience the same negative event (getting fired, being called a nigger), and yet one may find it very stressful whereas the other dismisses it. Theoretically, the event would have a negative psychological or health impact only on the individual who appraised (evaluated) the event as stressful. The events and appraisal approaches to measuring stress differ theoretically and substantively, and a good deal of debate has transpired regarding which is the superior approach (e.g., Cohen, 1986; Lazarus & Folkman, 1986). We believe that both approaches are beneficial and yield important but different information. Thus, when constructing the Schedule of Racist Events, we measured the frequency of various racist events *and* the appraisal of those events as stressful.

THE SCHEDULE OF
RACIST EVENTS (SRE)

The SRE is a brief self-report inventory consisting of 18 items to be rated on scales that range from 1 = *the event never happened* to 6 = *the event occurs almost all of the time.* Items assess the frequency of experiencing some specific racist event, as shown by the examples in Table 4.3. Each item is rated three times: once for the frequency of the event in the past year, once for the frequency of the event in one's entire life, and once for the appraisal of the event's stressfulness. These are summed to yield three total scores, Racist Events-Recent (sum of past year frequency ratings on all 18 items), Racist Events-Lifetime (sum of lifetime frequency ratings on all 18 items) and Racist Events-Appraisal (sum of all appraisal ratings) The internal-consistency reliabilities of these three 18-item scales for this sample were as follows: Racist Events-Recent Cronbach's alpha = .95, Racist Events-Lifetime α = .95, and Racist Events-Appraisal α = .93.

STUDY 5: ACCULTURATION,
RACISM, AND CIGARETTE SMOKING

PARTICIPANTS
AND MATERIALS

The 153 African American adults who participated in the previous study (Sample 3) participated in this study as well. In addition to the AAAS and a question about hypertension (described previously), subjects also completed the SRE and a question about smoking (Do You Smoke, yes or no). This permits us to examine smoking among this new sample and to investigate the role of acculturation versus racist events in smoking and in the hypertension found earlier among this sample.

TABLE 4.3 Sample Items From the Schedule of Racist Events

2. How many times have you been treated unfairly by your *employers, bosses and supervisors* because you are Black?

How many times in the past year?	1	2	3	4	5	6
How many times in your entire life?	1	2	3	4	5	6

How stressful was this for you?

Not at all stressful				Very stressful	
1	2	3	4	5	6

12. How many times did you *want to tell someone off for being racist but didn't say anything?*

How many times in the past year?	1	2	3	4	5	6
How many times in your entire life?	1	2	3	4	5	6

How stressful was this for you?

Not at all stressful				Very stressful	
1	2	3	4	5	6

14. How many times were you *forced to take drastic steps* (such as *filing a grievance, filing a lawsuit, quitting your job, moving away, and other actions*) to deal with some racist thing that was done to you?

How many times in the past year?	1	2	3	4	5	6
How many times in your entire life?	1	2	3	4	5	6

How stressful was this for you?

Not at all stressful				Very stressful	
1	2	3	4	5	6

15. How many times have you *been called a racist name like nigger, coon, jungle bunny or other names?*

How many times in the past year?	1	2	3	4	5	6
How many times in your entire life?	1	2	3	4	5	6

How stressful was this for you?

Not at all stressful				Very stressful	
1	2	3	4	5	6

RESULTS

Results for cigarette smoking and acculturation for this new sample (Sample 3) were significant, MANOVA Hotelling's $T^2 = 0.17$, Exact $F(8, 124) = 2.64$, $p = .01$): The smokers ($n = 24$) in this sample, like those in Study 3 (Sample 1), differed significantly from their nonsmoking colleagues ($n = 115$) on the AAAS: They were more traditional than those who did not smoke. As shown in the follow-up ANOVAs in Table 4.4, the smokers in this sample differed from the nonsmokers on only two AAAS subscales, whereas with the previous sample, differences on a greater number of subscales emerged. Subscale differences aside, however, the finding that smokers tend to be more traditional and nonsmokers more acculturated has been consistent across the two studies and the two different independent samples. The question, however, is whether the greater smoking among more traditional African Americans is related to more frequent experiences with racism.

To assess this, we conducted a MANOVA that compared the smokers and nonsmokers in this sample on their scores on the SRE with three dependent variables: Racist Events-Recent, -Lifetime, and -Appraisal. The MANOVA was significant, Hotelling's $T^2 = 0.101$, Exact $F(3, 123) = 4.16$, $p = .008$, indicating that smokers and nonsmokers differed in their scores on the SRE. The follow-up ANOVAs (shown in Table 4.5) indicated that smokers reported significantly more frequent racial discrimination throughout their lives than did nonsmokers (Racist Events-Lifetime) and also appraised racial discrimination as more stressful than did their nonsmoking counterparts.

These data lend support to the view that experiencing racist stress is related to smoking among African Americans, in that smokers not only reported more frequent racist events but also found those events to be more stressful than did nonsmokers. In addition, given that adult smokers typically began smoking early in life, between the ages of 10 and 20 years (Landrine, Klonoff, & Fritz, 1994), it makes sense that lifetime experience of racism (which includes early life) rather than recent (past year) experience of racism was related to smoking. Finally, although the sample was quite small and replication with larger samples is needed, such findings from a small sample are of considerable import. To find such strong, statistically significant results with so small a sample of smokers ($n = 24$) suggests that the relationship between racism and smoking for African Americans in the general population must be a large one, with a magnitude of effect so large that even our small sample possessed sufficient statistical power to be sensitive to that effect.

TABLE 4.4 Acculturation and Smoking Among a New Sample

AAAS Scale	Nonsmokers' Mean	Smokers' Mean	SS	F^a	p
Family	48.25	53.04	421.63	2.53	ns
Preference for Things Black	51.55	55.90	348.09	2.21	ns
Food	31.96	42.79	2156.30	11.58	.001
Interracial Attitudes	28.15	28.82	8.12	0.08	ns
Health	48.97	54.57	576.96	2.15	ns
Religion	32.40	31.18	27.41	0.31	ns
Socialization	43.16	49.55	749.19	4.16	.04
Superstition	17.95	20.91	161.21	2.99	ns
Total AAAS Scale	302.38	336.76	$t(131) = -2.35^b$		.02

a. $df = (1, 131)$ for each F above.
b. This t-test on the total score was conducted separately.

TABLE 4.5 Comparing Smokers and Nonsmokers on Schedule of Racist Events

Racist Events Scale	Nonsmokers' Mean	Smokers' Mean	SS	F[a]	p
Racist Events-Recent	42.46	44.66	94.38	0.22	ns
Racist Events-Lifetime	51.14	62.61	2560.94	5.47	.02
Racist Events-Appraisal	50.11	61.53	2540.15	5.47	.02

a. $df = (1, 125)$ for each F above.

108   AFRICAN AMERICAN ACCULTURATION

The questions remaining, however, are,

1. Do more traditional African Americans experience more racism than their acculturated counterparts?
2. Is it this racism—rather than being traditional—that accounts for their smoking?

To answer the first question, we ran a cluster analysis of cases, shown in Table 4.6. In cluster analysis, a set of dependent variables of interest (acculturation, Racist Events-Lifetime, Racist Events-Recent, and Racist Events-Appraisal) are entered, and the program then generates groups (clusters) of subjects from the sample who differ on the variables. If subjects can be grouped by all of the variables because the variables "hang together," then statistically significant differences between the clusters on all of the variables will be found. If, however, a particular variable is not associated with cluster membership, then no significant differences on that variable will emerge. Cluster analysis (CA) is similar to MANOVA; the difference is that in CA, the program defines the groups whereas in MANOVA the researcher defines the groups.

In the first cluster analysis, we requested two groups who differed significantly on the variables, and in the second analysis we requested three. If level of acculturation is associated with amount of racism experienced, then the clusters should differ significantly on both of these types of variables. As shown in Table 4.6, this indeed was the case.

In the two-cluster analysis (top of Table 4.6), the clusters differed on Total AAAS, on Racist Events-Lifetime, and on Racist Events-Recent, but they did not differ in the appraisal of racist events as stressful. We called the first cluster *acculturated* because of their low scores on the AAAS, and the second *traditional* because of their high scores (*100 points higher* than the former) on the AAAS. It is clear that traditional African Americans experienced more frequent racial discrimination in the past year, as well as throughout their lives, and that this was not a function of evaluating the events differently—both traditional

TABLE 4.6 Cluster Analysis of Cases: Acculturation and Racist Events

Two Clusters	Cluster 1 (Acculturated) n = 69	Cluster 2 (Traditional) n = 57	MS	F^a	p
Total AAAS Score	257.84	360.57	332059.18	225.77	.0001
Racist Events-Lifetime	48.37	60.26	4408.17	9.41	.003
Racist Events-Recent	39.95	47.11	1600.76	3.90	.05
Racist Events-Appraisal	49.58	56.15	1350.26	2.83	.095 ns

Three Clusters	Cluster 1 (Acculturated) n = 22	Cluster 2 (Unknown) n = 60	Cluster 3 (Traditional) n = 46	MS	F^b	p
Total AAAS Score	238.78	322.60	398.29	205862.099	225.72	.0001
Racist Events-Lifetime	47.09	54.02	66.78	2888.49	6.24	.003
Racist Events-Recent	40.39	42.44	49.03	564.48	1.35	ns

NOTE: ns = not significant.
a. $df = 1$, 124 for each F.
b. $df = 2$, 125 for each F.

and acculturated subjects evaluated racism as equally stressful (appraisal). In the three-cluster analysis (bottom of Table 4.6), we omitted Racist Events-Appraisal because it was not significant in the prior analysis. In the three-cluster case, the nature of the relationship between acculturation and racism is highlighted as a linear one: As traditionality increases (left to right across the clusters), so too does racial discrimination against the African Americans in question. As acculturation scores increase from acculturated to traditional, both Lifetime and Recent Racist Events increased (although the effect for the latter was not significant).

These data provide support for the hypothesis that traditional African Americans are perceived as being "more Black" than their acculturated counterparts and consequently experience more racial discrimination. These effects cannot be said to be an artifact of the social class, gender, age, or educational level of the traditional African Americans because the data presented in Chapter 3 indicate that these sociological variables are unrelated to scores on the AAAS. Likewise, these results cannot be said to be an artifact of differences in the appraisal of events, for both traditional and acculturated African Americans evaluated racial discrimination as equally stressful. Thus these data suggest that the punishment from European Americans for remaining immersed in African American culture (as opposed to rejecting it in favor of the dominant culture and becoming acculturated) is increased racial discrimination. Although the small sample here remains a limitation of this study, it is also the case that to find such large effects for racism and acculturation with samples so small suggests that these effects are powerful and large in the population. Thus, these data suggest that traditional and acculturated African Americans are treated very differently in the world, that is, that levels of African American acculturation may predict life circumstances and treatment and these in turn may predict physical and mental health.

The final question remaining is whether traditional African Americans smoke because they are traditional, or because they

TABLE 4.7   Logistic Regression Predicting Smoking From Acculturation
and Racist Events

Step Number	Variable Selected	B	Wald	df	Significance	R
1.	Racist Events-Lifetime	.061	11.45	1	.0007	.29
2.	Racist Events-Recent	−.046	6.03	1	.01	−.19
	Constant	−3.04	17.31	1	.00005	

experience greater racism than their nonsmoking, more acculturated counterparts—with this racism mediated by their traditionality (as the data in Table 4.6 suggest). To provide a preliminary
answer to this question, we ran a logistic regression analysis.
Logistic regression is a type of stepwise, multiple regression in
which the outcome variable to be predicted is categorical (yes/no;
present/absent; smoker/nonsmoker) rather than a continuous
score. Membership in one category (smoker) rather than the other
(nonsmoker) of the dependent variable is predicted from the
weighted, linear combination of predictors, as in ordinary regression, and the most powerful predictor of category membership is
selected first by the program.

If smoking among African Americans is a response to racist
stress rather than to traditionality, then (a) racist events should
be selected first in the logistic regression as the best predictor of
smoking, and (b) acculturation, hypothesized to mediate racist
events, should not be selected as a predictor at all. Thus, subjects
were coded as smokers versus nonsmokers, and this category
membership was then predicted from four independent variables:
total Racist Events-Lifetime score, Racist Events-Recent score,
Racist Events-Appraisal score, and Total AAAS score. These results
are shown in Table 4.7.

As indicated in the table, Racist Events-Lifetime was selected
as the best predictor of smoking versus nonsmoking (and had a
positive correlation), followed by Racist Events-Recent (which
had a negative correlation); acculturation (as hypothesized) was
not selected as a predictor at all. About 97% of cases (smoker
versus nonsmoker) were correctly classified as such based solely

on Lifetime and Recent Racist Events as predictors; although the correlations appear at first to be small, in fact, this is an extraordinarily high rate of accurate categorization based on a mere two predictors.

These data are consistent with the hypothesis that traditional African Americans experience more racial discrimination (racist stress) than their acculturated counterparts and that this racist stress then in part predicts and accounts for the greater smoking among traditional African Americans. The relationship among these variables may be one in which level of African American acculturation predicts racism, and racism predicts smoking. A study with a larger sample and using a hierarchical path analysis is needed to verify this model in which acculturation is a distal (indirect) predictor of smoking and racism a proximal (direct, causal) predictor of smoking. We encourage such a study.

STUDY 6: ACCULTURATION, RACISM, AND HYPERTENSION

In Study 4, we found that African Americans reporting hypertension ($n = 22$) were more traditional than their normotensive ($n = 115$) counterparts. We again speculated that traditionality mediated racism, and that racism (pent-up anger about it in particular) accounted for hypertension; we tested this hypothesis in Study 6.

To assess this hypothesis, we ran a MANOVA comparing the two blood-pressure groups on their scores on Racist Events-Lifetime, Racist Events-Recent, and Racist Events-Appraisal. This MANOVA was significant, Hotelling's $T^2 = 0.114$, Exact $F(3, 123) = 4.66$, $p = .004$, indicating that the blood-pressure groups differed in their experience with racism. The follow-up ANOVAs are shown in Table 4.8. These revealed that the hypertensive group reported more frequent racial discrimination throughout their lives than did their normotensive counterparts, and they also appraised racial discrimination as more stressful.

TABLE 4.8 ANOVA of Blood Pressure and Racist Events

Racist Events Scale	Normal Blood-Pressure Group Mean	High Blood-Pressure Group Mean	SS	F[a]	p
Racist Events-Recent	42.12	46.68	363.23	0.89	ns
Racist Events-Lifetime	51.58	62.05	1921.23	4.06	.046
Racist Events-Appraisal	49.59	65.79	4601.51	10.28	.002

a. $df = (1, 125)$ for each F above.

113

We then ran a logistic regression analysis, with blood pressure as the outcome variable (high v. normal), and with four independent variables as predictors: Racist Events-Recent, Racist Events-Lifetime, Racist Events-Appraisal, and total AAAS scores. We predicted again that racist events would be the best predictor of blood pressure and that acculturation would not be related to hypertension, once racism was taken into account. These results are shown in Table 4.9.

As hypothesized, acculturation was not selected as a predictor of hypertension when racism was included in the analysis. Instead, the only predictor of hypertension versus normal blood pressure was Racist Events-Appraisal. Hypertension was not related to the frequency of racist events. Rather, hypertensives were subjects who evaluated racist events as very stressful, and normotensives (experiencing those same racist events) were subjects who evaluated them as less stressful; the (physical and psychological) impact of racist events was more severe for hypertensives than for normotensives. Although the correlation again appears to be small, all cases of hypertensives versus normotensives were correctly categorized as such, using Racist Events-Appraisal as the sole predictor.

OVERALL DISCUSSION

In studies entailing two different samples, we found consistently that smokers tended to be more traditional than their nonsmoking cohorts. The additional analyses here, however, strongly suggest that the relationship between acculturation and smoking among African Americans is a function of racism; traditional African Americans experience more racial discrimination and smoke cigarettes, whereas their more acculturated counterparts experience significantly less discrimination and do not smoke. Likewise, being traditional also was related to hypertension, and further analyses revealed that this too could be understood as a result of racism.

TABLE 4.9   Logistic Regression Predicting Hypertension From
                 Acculturation and Racist Events

Step Number	Variable Selected	B	Wald	df	Significance	R
1.	Racist Events-Appraisal	.03	8.28	1	.004	.24
	Constant	-3.46	21.56	1	.0005	

Although these findings were the product of a large number of analyses conducted on small samples, we believe that these results are not spurious. This is because the significant differences that emerged were consistent across the samples, were highly significant despite the small sample size (suggesting large effects in the population), and were fully predicted from a specific hypothesis and model. Replication with larger samples is nonetheless essential to a full understanding of the role of racism and acculturation in African American health, with hierarchical path analyses (establishing causal relationships) crucial to those demonstrations.

These preliminary data suggest that both acculturation and racism play a role in African American health status and health behavior, and so these factors must be included in future research, as well as in the design of effective health promotion and disease prevention programs for African Americans. Another important finding suggested by these data is that level of acculturation predicts racism, and that this relationship is a linear one in which,[1] as traditionality increases, racism too increases. Such a finding is of enormous significance, with serious implications for African American physical and mental health as well as implications for civil litigation. That is, if racism (racist stress) indeed causes hypertension and smoking among African Americans, and these in turn (as the empirical literature indicates) cause stroke, heart disease, cancer, death from these conditions, and drug abuse, then racist individuals and institutions are legally liable for the deleterious health consequences of racial discrimination. Studies examining the relationship between racism and chronic physical conditions among African Americans (hypertension, cancer) are needed to clarify these findings, and we have such a study currently under way.

AN ADDITIONAL, POTENTIALLY
IMPORTANT VARIABLE: SKIN COLOR

Given the importance of data suggesting that acculturation predicts racism and that racism predicts smoking and hypertension among African Americans, our interpretation of these data must be carefully considered. Specifically, one additional variable that could, theoretically, be related to racism, hypertension, and smoking is skin color, and this variable must be considered and evaluated, as follows.

Some studies suggest that darker-skinned African Americans experience more discrimination and a lower social evaluation than their lighter-skinned counterparts (e.g., Boyd-Franklin, 1989b; Neal & Wilson, 1989; Okazawa-Rey, Robinson, & Ward, 1987; Robinson & Ward, 1995); this could, theoretically, be related to smoking. Likewise, other studies have found that dark-skinned African Americans are more likely than their light-skinned counterparts to have hypertension; they tend to have significantly higher blood pressure than their light-skinned cohorts (Gentry, Chesney, Gary, Hall, & Harburg, 1982; Harburg et al., 1973), with this blood pressure related to greater discrimination against them and to greater, subsequent anger. How, then, does skin color figure in the relationship among acculturation, racism, and hypertension and smoking? Are acculturated African Americans treated better (with less racism) than their more traditional counterparts because they seem more White—more similar culturally to European Americans and therefore less threatening to the status quo? Or are acculturated African Americans *lighter-skinned* than their traditional counterparts, and do they experience less racism because of that, with level of acculturation actually not related to racism? Perhaps light-skinned African Americans are afforded greater opportunities to acculturate because they are light-skinned, with light skin predicting level of acculturation, level of acculturation predicting racism, and racism predicting physical and mental health. Does skin color mediate traditionality and traditionality then mediate racism? Or is the relationship between skin color and racism a direct one in which acculturation plays no role? If skin color (race per se) is directly related to racism and racism related to health, then our thesis that culture—not race per se—is the most important variable in African American life is seriously overstated. If, however, skin color (race per se) is not related directly to racism but instead is related only to acculturation (with acculturation directly related to racism and health), then the final proof for the primacy of culture is established. Thus, we add skin color to the picture and investigate its role below.

STUDY 7: ACCULTURATION, SKIN COLOR, DISCRIMINATION, AND PHYSICAL HEALTH

Thus far, we have seen that traditional African Americans reported experiencing racial discrimination significantly more frequently than did their more acculturated counterparts, and we raised questions about the extent to which this might be a function of skin color. We explore those relationships below.

PARTICIPANTS, PROCEDURE, AND MATERIALS

The 153 African Americans (Sample 3) who participated in the previous study were involved in this one, as well; they have been described elsewhere. These subjects completed a questionnaire that was detailed earlier in this chapter. However, in addition to the AAAS, SRE, and other questions, these subjects also were asked to rate their skin color on a scale that ranged from 1 = *very light-skinned* to 5 = *very dark-skinned*.

RESULTS

The first question is whether skin color is related to acculturation and, specifically, whether traditional African Americans tend to be darker-skinned than their more acculturated counterparts. To answer this, we divided the subjects into three skin-color groups. The Light-Skin Group was the 24 subjects who rated their skin color as 1 or 2 (very light-skinned and light-skinned, respectively). The Medium-Skin Group was the 70 subjects who rated their skin color as 3 (medium-skinned), and, the Dark-Skin Group was the 43 subjects who rated their skin color a 4 or 5 (dark-skinned, and very dark-skinned, respectively). Five subjects did not answer the question (some were light- and others dark-skinned but all of them extremely angry about this skin-color question), and so they were excluded from the analyses.

Acculturation and Skin Color

A MANOVA, with these three skin color groups and the subscales of the AAAS as dependent variables, was conducted and was significant, Hotelling's T^2 = 0.229, $F(16, 244)$=1.75, p = .039, indicating that the skin-color groups differed in their levels of acculturation. Follow-up ANOVAs and post hoc Tukey comparisons (shown in Table 4.10) revealed that dark-skinned and medium-skinned subjects scored more traditional than light-skinned subjects on the Foods, Religion, and total AAAS score, and that dark-skinned subjects also scored as more traditional than their light-skinned counterparts on the Health and Childhood subscales as well. That is, dark-skinned subjects scored higher (more traditional) than light-skinned subjects on four of the subscales, as well as on the total AAAS score. Some of these differences were quite large (e.g., an 11-point difference on the very brief Foods subscale, and a 52.71 point difference on the total AAAS score), and their statistical significance thereby is unlikely to be spurious.

TABLE 4.10 African American Acculturation and Skin Color

AAAS Scale	Light-Skinned Group Mean	Medium-Skinned Group Mean	Dark-Skinned Group Mean	SS	F^a	p
Family	46.85	48.82	50.26	176.799	0.51	ns
Preference for Things Black	51.13	51.70	53.37	99.39	0.29	ns
Food	24.50	35.58	36.56	2603.01	7.13	.001
Interracial Attitudes	25.85	28.11	29.49	199.92	1.04	ns
Health	41.21	49.95	55.03	2893.41	5.78	.004
Religion	26.67	33.06	33.70	875.92	5.28	.006
Socialization	38.65	44.33	47.63	1219.92	3.48	.034
Superstition	17.83	18.06	19.37	53.81	0.49	ns
Total AAAS Scale	272.69	309.61	325.40	42512.67^b	5.51	.005

NOTE: ns = not significant; Post hoc Tukeys at α = .05: for Health and Socialization Scales, Dark-Skinned > Light-Skinned, for Food, Religion, and Total AAAS Scale score, Dark-Skinned and Medium-Skinned > Light-Skinned.
a. $df = (2, 130)$ for each F above.
b. This one-way ANOVA $(df = 2, 130)$ on the total score was conducted separately.

These findings suggest that there is a relationship between skin color and level of acculturation among African Americans. To gain a preliminary sense of the strength of that relationship, we ran a simple chi-square using the two skin-color groups (light v. dark) and two levels of acculturation (high-traditional v. low-acculturated), with the latter defined by a median split using the sample's median on the total AAAS score. This chi-square was significant, $\chi^2 (1) = 7.49, p = .006$. The associated phi coefficient (a correlation for categorical data) was $\phi = .34$ $(p = .006)$. Thus about 11.5% of the variance (the correlation squared) in acculturation among African Americans is accounted for by skin color. Although this finding is statistically significant and intriguing, the strength of the relationship between skin color and acculturation is not as strong as the MANOVA might suggest. Nonetheless, 11.5% of the variance is a fair proportion, which no doubt has practical significance. Thus future studies of this phenomenon are needed to clarify and explain the relationship.

The next question is whether traditional African Americans experience more frequent racial discrimination because they are traditional (cultural racism) or because they tend to be dark-skinned (simplistic, garden-variety racism). Although we lack a sufficient sample size to answer this question in the most statistically powerful and persuasive manner (e.g., a hierarchial path analysis), there are two analyses that can provide a preliminary answer to this question.

Acculturation, Racist
Events, and Skin Color

First, we can divide subjects into skin-color groups and assess differences between those groups on the AAAS and on the three subscales of the SRE. If racial discrimination is a reaction to skin color alone, then the skin-color groups should differ on the SRE scales but not on the AAAS. Thus subjects were divided into light-skinned (ratings of 1 and 2, $n = 24$) and dark-skinned (ratings of 4 and 5, $n = 43$), and a MANOVA was conducted using Racist

Events-Recent, Racist Events-Lifetime, Racist Events-Appraisal, and total AAAS score as dependent variables. This MANOVA was significant, $T^2 = 0.219$, $F(4, 55) = 3.12$, $p = .025$. Follow-up ANOVAs, shown in Table 4.11, revealed, however, that the skin-color groups did not differ in their experiences of racism, but instead, only differed in their levels of acculturation, with dark-skinned subjects being more traditional. Racism experienced by these African Americans was not related to being light- or dark-skinned.

This tentatively suggests that the greater racism experienced by traditional African Americans probably is not a response to the fact that they tend to be darker skinned (ordinary racism) but is instead a response to their traditionality (cultural racism). This implies that perhaps the relationship among skin color, racism, and acculturation is that skin color in part predicts level of acculturation, and level of acculturation in part predicts racism experienced, with no direct relationship between skin color and racism experienced. Thus, the second way that we can explore these relationships is to calculate the correlations among racist events, skin color (entered as a continuous variable of 1 to 5), and acculturation; we predict significant r's between skin color and acculturation, and between acculturation and racist events, but no significant correlation between skin color and racism. These data are shown in Table 4.12.

As shown in Table 4.12, skin color was significantly and positively correlated with level of acculturation, but it was not related to Racist Events-Recent, Racist Events-Lifetime, or Racist Events-Appraisal. Instead, level of acculturation alone was related to these three measures of racial discrimination.

DISCUSSION

These data, when considered in the context of the data reported previously, suggest that acculturation is a strong predictor of the amount of racism African Americans experience and that racism is a strong predictor of health-related problems, such as smoking

TABLE 4.11 ANOVA of Acculturation and Racist Events for Skin-Color Groups

Scales	Light-Skinned Group Mean	Dark-Skinned Group Mean	SS	F^a	p
Racist Events-Recent	39.12	44.63	430.86	1.01	ns
Racist Events-Lifetime	45.76	53.60	871.57	1.72	ns
Racist Events-Appraisal	46.97	52.04	363.95	0.76	ns
Total AAAS Score	270.50	323.12	39,263.88	11.24	.001

NOTE: ns = not significant.
a. $df = (1, 58)$ for each F above.

TABLE 4.12 Correlation Matrix of Acculturation, Skin Color, and Racist Events

	Total AAAS	Racist Events-Recent	Racist Events-Lifetime	Racist Events-Appraisal
Skin Color	.27***	.09[a]	.14[a]	.08[a]
Total AAAS Score		.19*	.32****	.25**

a. not significant.
*$p = .026$; **$p = .005$; ***$p = .001$; ****$p = .0001$.

123

124

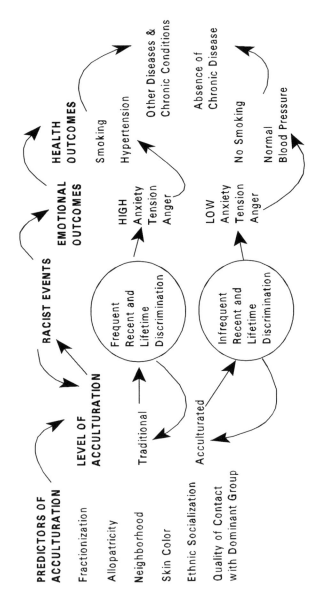

Figure 4.1. Theoretical and Empirical Relationships Among Variables

and hypertension. In addition, skin color is related to acculturation, with some (but certainly not all) traditional African Americans tending to be darker-skinned than their more acculturated counterparts. Skin color accounted for only 11.5% of the variance in level of acculturation, however. Although the skin color-acculturation relationship is worthy of investigation, the majority of the variance in level of acculturation is likely to be explained by the factors detailed in Chapter 2. The nature of these relationships is summarized in Figure 4.1.

With these preliminary data on the relationship between acculturation and physical health among African Americans established, we can now turn to a similar analysis of the role of acculturation in mental health among African Americans.

NOTE

1. Level of acculturation (being traditional) may predict racism, as our data suggest. Likewise, however, racism also may predict level of acculturation, with acculturated African Americans who have experienced racism returning to neo-traditionality as theorized in the principle of return discussed in Chapter 2. Both directions (racism ↔ traditionality) may apply.

5

Acculturation and Mental Health

Numerous studies have demonstrated that stress plays a major role in psychiatric symptoms for people in general (Dohrenwend & Dohrenwend, 1981; Lazarus, 1966) and for African Americans as well (Brown & Gary, 1987; Dohrenwend & Dohrenwend, 1970; Dressler, 1986; Neff & Husaini, 1980). The strength of the relationship between stress and symptoms for African Americans is in part mediated by social class, with low social class acting as an additional source of stress (Dohrenwend & Dohrenwend, 1970; Dressler, 1986; Neff & Husaini, 1980). The stress-symptom relationship also is mediated by social support and strong family ties (Brown & Gary, 1987; Dressler, 1980, 1985a; Ellinson, 1990; Giffith, 1985; Hays, 1973), as well as by coping skills (Dressler, 1980, 1985b; Neighbors, Jackson, & Bowman, 1983): African Americans who have strong social support networks and family ties, and/or a diversity of coping skills, exhibit fewer stress-related symptoms (such as anxiety and depression) than those who lack these resources. This stress-coping-symptom relationship is undoubtedly affected by level of acculturation for African Americans as it is for other minority groups (e.g., Latinos). Acculturation, theoretically, may play a large role in the type of coping used, as well as in the impact of stressful life events, and thus in stress-related symptoms exhibited. In this chapter, we explore the relationships among stress, coping, acculturation, and psychiatric symptoms for African Americans.

STUDY 8

PARTICIPANTS AND MATERIALS

The data reported here are from Sample 3 (described elsewhere) and entail analyses of the remaining questionnaires and instruments completed by that sample. In addition to the AAAS, the Schedule of Racist Events (SRE), and a question on skin color, these participants also completed the following:

1. The Hopkins Symptom Checklist (HSCL-58; Derogatis, Lipman, Rickles, Uhlenhuth, & Covi, 1974), measuring five types of psychiatric symptoms (Anxiety, Depression, Obsessive-Compulsive, Interpersonal Sensitivity, and Somatization) and yielding a total Symptom Score as well;
2. The PERI-LES (Dohrenwend et al., 1978), measuring the frequency of specific, generic life events presumed to be stressful for all people (e.g., getting fired) and yielding a single score;
3. The Perceived Stress Scale (PSS; Cohen et al., 1983), measuring the appraisal (evaluation) of specific situations as stressful and yielding a single score; and
4. The Ways of Coping questionnaire (WOC; Lazarus & Folkman, 1984), which assesses the use of eight distinct coping strategies and yields eight scores.

The WOC measures the following coping strategies (Folkman, Lazarus, Dunkel-Schetter, DeLongis, & Gruen, 1986):

1. *Confrontative coping*, characterized by aggressive efforts to change the situation, for example, "I stood my ground and fought for what I wanted"
2. *Seeking social support*, characterized by obtaining emotional support from others, for example, "I asked a friend or relative I respected for advice"
3. *Planful problem solving*, characterized by problem-focused efforts to solve the situation, for example, "I made a plan of action and followed it"
4. *Self-control*, characterized by efforts to regulate one's feelings, for example, "I tried to keep my feelings to myself"
5. *Distancing*, characterized by efforts to detach oneself from the source of stress or stressful situation, for example, "I didn't let it get to me, refused to think too much about it"
6. *Positive reappraisal*, characterized by efforts to find positive meaning in the experience, for example, "I came out of the experience better than when I went in"
7. *Accepting responsibility*, which consists of acknowledging one's role in the problem, for example, "I criticized or lectured myself"
8. *Escape-avoidance*, which consists of wishful thinking or efforts to avoid or escape the situation, for example, "I wished that I could change what had happened or how I felt"

HYPOTHESIS 1

The first question is: Do levels of acculturation among African Americans play a role in psychiatric symptoms? We hypothesized that levels of African American acculturation do play a role in such symptoms and play an important one. Thus, we hypothesized that African American acculturation would account for additional variance in symptoms among this population, above and beyond the variance accounted for by social class, skin color, generic stress, and racism. In other words, we hypothesized that knowing about acculturation would significantly increase our ability to predict symptoms among African Americans.

To assess the hypothesis that acculturation accounts for a portion of the variance in African Americans' symptoms that is not accounted for by social class (income and education), generic stressors, skin color, and racism, a hierarchical regression analysis was conducted as follows.

1. We entered social class (measured as education and income) —the typical predictor of symptoms for African Americans—on the first step; a statistically significant change in R^2 resulting from these variables would yield information on how much variance, if any, in African Americans' symptoms is accounted for by social class alone.

2. Then, we entered skin color (measured on a scale from 1 to 5) on the second step, and a significant change in R^2 would mean that skin color accounted for additional variance above and beyond that accounted for by social class.

3. Next, we entered scores on the PERI-LES (a measure of the frequency of stressors) on the third step, with a significant change in R^2 meaning that generic stressors account for variance in symptoms not accounted for by class and skin color.[1]

4. Next, we entered racism on the fourth step (Racist Events-Lifetime, -Recent, and -Appraisal) to examine the extent to which racism would account for additional variance in symptoms above and beyond the traditional predictors (social class and generic stressors) and skin color.

5. Finally, on the last step, we entered total scores on the AAAS. A significant change in R^2 resulting from entering the AAAS last in the regression would mean that acculturation accounts for unique variance in African Americans' symptoms, above and beyond, and not accounted for by, social class, generic stressors, and culturally specific stressors (racism) and variables (skin color). In addition, if the R^2 for acculturation exceeds that for any of the variables entered on the prior steps, then acculturation not only accounts for additional variance in symptoms but also accounts for more of the variance in, and is a better predictor of,

TABLE 5.1 Hierarchical Regression Predicting Total Psychiatric Symptoms Hopkins Symptom Checklist Total Score: AAAS Entered Last

Step	Variable(s) Entered	R	R^2	Change in R^2	F of Change	Significance of F
1	Education and income	.135	.018	.018	0.676	.51
2	Skin color	.254	.064	.046	3.56	.063
3	PERI-LES	.266	.071	.006	0.492	.485
4	Racist Events-Life, -Recent, -Appraisal	.399	.159	.088	2.36	.078
5	AAAS	.553	.306	.137	14.16	.0004

Overall ANOVA: SS = 15567.66; $F(8, 67) = 3.69, p < .0013$

the symptoms than is the prior variable. The results of this hierarchical regression are shown in Table 5.1.[2]

RESULTS

As shown in Table 5.1, social class accounted for a nonsignificant (significance of F shown in righthand column) 1.8% of the variance (Change in R^2 column) in symptoms; even though it was entered first, it played no role in symptoms. Skin color, on the other hand, entered on the second step, alone accounted for 4.6% of the variance in symptoms (Change in R^2 column) but this effect did not quite reach statistical significance (Significance of F column), perhaps because of the small sample size. Generic life events and stressors (PERI-LES), entered on the third step, clearly played no role in symptoms (0.6% of the variance in Change in R^2 column) with the effect of such stressors being as inconsequential as that of social class. Racism may account for 8.8% of the variance in symptoms, however (Change in R^2 column), and with a larger sample, this result may reach significance. Finally, acculturation, entered on the last step, accounted for 13.7% of the variance in symptoms (Change in R^2 column) and that effect was significant. Of all of the predictors entered, only acculturation accounted for a statistically significant (Significance of F column) amount of the variance (Change in R^2 column) in psychiatric symptoms among African Americans.

As hypothesized then, acculturation accounted for variance in psychiatric symptoms not accounted for by social class, skin color, racism, and generic stressors, and indeed, it accounted for more of the variance in symptoms than these typical (class, generic stressors) and culturally specific (skin color, racism) variables alone and combined. In addition, only the effects for skin color and racism approached statistical significance as predictors of symptoms, whereas the effects for social class and generic stressors did not; effects for the culturally specific predictors (skin color and racism) might have reached significance with a larger sample.

Table 5.1 suggests that acculturation accounts for 13.7% of the variance in African Americans' symptoms above and beyond the variance accounted for by class, generic stressors, skin color, and racism. Racism, however, is not a typical predictor of symptoms among African Americans (although it certainly needs to be).

Thus, to gain a preliminary sense of the percentage of variance accounted for by acculturation when racism has not been taken into account, we conducted a similar, hierarchical regression but entered acculturation on the next to the last step, and racism on the last step, as shown in Table 5.2. Again, social class (Step 1), skin color (Step 2), and generic stressors (Step 3) did not account for a significant percentage of the variance in psychiatric symptoms. Instead, acculturation (Step 4) accounted for 21.1% of the variance above and beyond that accounted for by the prior predictors. Racism, on the other hand, did not contribute significantly to symptoms once level of acculturation had been taken into account.

Thus, acculturation plays a large role—and perhaps the largest role of any single variable—in psychiatric symptoms among African Americans, accounting for 13.7% to 21.1% of the variance in those symptoms, above and beyond any variance accounted for by social class and generic stressors. This suggests that psychiatric symptoms among African Americans perhaps cannot be predicted or understood without taking acculturation into

TABLE 5.2 Hierarchical Regression Predicting Total Psychiatric Symptoms: AAAS Entered Next to Last Outcome: Hopkins Symptom Checklist Total Score

Step	Variable(s) Entered	R	R^2	Change in R^2	F of Change	Significance of F
1	Education and income	.135	.018	.018	0.676	.51
2	Skin color	.254	.064	.046	3.56	.063
3	PERI-LES	.266	.071	.006	0.492	.485
4	AAAS	.53	.282	.211	20.53	.00005
5	Racist Events-Life, -Recent, -Appraisal	.553	.306	.024	.771	.514

Overall ANOVA: SS = 15567.66; $F(8, 67) = 3.69, p < .0013$

account. This, in turn, raises the possibility that the predictors of symptoms for African Americans vary with level of acculturation; stressors may have different impacts on acculturated versus traditional African Americans, and coping styles used by these two groups also may be different, with both of these mediating symptoms. Thus, acculturation-specific statistical models of symptoms among African Americans may be needed and may reveal unique predictors of symptoms for acculturated versus traditional African Americans. If such models reveal such differences, then this would mean that (a) traditional and acculturated African Americans must be approached and understood as separate, unique, sociocultural groups where psychiatric symptoms are concerned and that (b) different therapies, focusing on the specific, best predictors of symptoms for each group, may be needed for acculturated versus traditional African Americans. We turn our attention to this important possibility.

HYPOTHESIS 2

We hypothesized that the best predictors of psychiatric symptoms for acculturated African Americans would differ from the best predictors of those symptoms for traditional African Americans, with generic stressors having differential impacts and different coping styles being used by and playing a role in the symptoms of the two groups. To explore this hypothesis, we divided the subjects into two groups based on their scores on the AAAS. The *Traditional Group* consisted of the 68 subjects who scored above the sample median of 306.00 on the AAAS; their range of scores on the AAAS was 307 to 518 (Mean = 358.55, σ = 37.06). The *Acculturated Group* was the 67 subjects who scored below the sample median of 306.00 on the AAAS; their range of scores on the AAAS was 151 to 304 (Mean = 254.68, σ = 38.03). Thus, the average (mean) score for the two acculturation groups on the AAAS differed by 100 points (the total N here, 135, does not sum to 153 because some subjects failed to complete portions of the instruments).

We then ran a series of stepwise regression analyses for the acculturated and then the traditional African American groups. Each regression predicted a specific symptom as measured by the Hopkins Symptom Checklist (e.g., Total Symptoms, Depression, Somatization Symptoms, etc.) as the outcome variable. Predictors entered for each and every regression were: skin color; scores on the PERI-LES (frequency of generic stressors); scores on the PSS (appraisal of generic stressors); income (treated as a measure of social class), and scores on the eight different coping styles measured by the WOC. Stepwise regression selects the best predictors of symptoms (in order of their predictive power) and does not select variables that are poor predictors. If symptoms for traditional and acculturated African Americans are predicted by different variables as hypothesized, then the stepwise regressions for the two acculturation groups should differ. These results are shown in Table 5.3.

As indicated in Table 5.3, three of the six symptoms (Total Symptoms, Depression, and Somatic symptoms) of acculturated African Americans were best predicted by using the Taking Responsibility (self-blaming) coping style, with appraised generic stress (PSS) an additional factor. The remaining types of symptoms for acculturated African Americans (i.e., Obsessive-Compulsive symptoms, Interpersonal Sensitivity symptoms [low self-esteem,

TABLE 5.3 Stepwise Regressions Selecting Best Predictors of
            Psychiatric Symptoms for Acculturated Versus
            Traditional African Americans

Variable Selected	R	R^2	SS	(df)F	Significance of F
Symptom: Total Hopkins Score					
Acculturated					
Step 1 Responsibility	.611	.374	6921.56	(1, 28)16.72	.0003
Step 2 PSS	.704	.495	9169.14	(2, 27)13.24	.0001
Traditional					
Step 1 Escape-Avoid	.594	.353	3458.45	(1, 21)11.47	.003
Symptom: Hopkins Depression Score					
Acculturated					
Step 1 Responsibility	.635	.404	423.37	(1, 29)19.63	.0001
Step 2 PSS	.743	.551	578.04	(2, 28)17.19	.00005
Traditional					
Step 1 Escape-Avoid	.600	.360	262.56	(1, 34)19.14	.0001
Step 2 PSS	.666	.444	323.77	(2, 33)13.18	.0001
Step 3 Distancing	.713	.508	370.50	(3, 32)11.02	.00005
Symptom: Hopkins Somatization Score					
Acculturated					
Step 1 Responsibility	.502	.252	263.27	(1, 30)10.12	.0034
Traditional					
Step 1 Escape-Avoid	.454	.206	286.92	(1, 34)8.83	.005
Step 2 Social Support	.591	.349	486.22	(2, 33)8.86	.008
Symptom: Hopkins Obsessive-Compulsive Score					
Acculturated					
Step 1 Escape-Avoid	.574	.329	169.84	(1, 33)16.18	.0003
Step 2 Self-Control	.646	.418	215.56	(2, 32)11.47	.0002
Step 3 PSS	.699	.489	252.21	(3, 31)9.87	.0001
Traditional					
Step 1 PSS	.451	.203	155.76	(1, 31)7.92	.008
Step 2 Distancing	.553	.305	233.83	(2, 30)6.59	.004
Symptom: Hopkins Interpersonal Sensitivity Score					
Acculturated					
Step 1 Escape-Avoid	.582	.338	124.53	(1, 31)15.84	.0004
Step 2 PSS	.649	.422	155.43	(2, 30)10.96	.0003
Traditional					
Step 1 Escape-Avoid	.652	.425	152.11	(1, 32)23.69	.00005
Symptom: Hopkins Anxiety Score					
Acculturated					
Step 1 Escape-Avoid	.598	.358	132.76	(1, 32)17.85	.0002
Traditional					
Step 1 Escape-Avoid	.685	.469	66.79	(1, 30)26.48	.00005

feelings of inadequacy], and symptoms on the Anxiety subscale) were predicted by using the Escape-Avoidance coping style. In each case, the R^2 was large, with 25.2% to 50.1% of the variance in the symptoms of acculturated subjects accounted for with one or two predictors. For traditional subjects, nearly every type of symptom—with the exception of Obsessive-Compulsive symptoms—was best predicted by the Escape-Avoidance (i.e., deny the problem) coping style, with additional variance accounted for by the Distancing coping style (another way of denying the problem) and by appraised, generic stress (PSS). For the traditional subjects, too, the R^2s were large, with 30.5% to 50.8% of the variance in symptoms accounted for by a few predictors.

DISCUSSION

We found in this preliminary study that an enormous percentage of the variance in psychiatric symptoms among African Americans could be explained if African Americans are separated into and analyzed as different acculturation groups. Specifically, we found that the best predictors of psychiatric symptoms for acculturated African Americans differ from those for their traditional counterparts. Acculturated subjects tended to blame themselves for problems (Taking Responsibility coping style) whereas traditional subjects tended to deny problems (Escape-Avoidance, Distancing coping styles), with both of these maladaptive coping styles predicting psychiatric symptoms. Likewise, appraised, generic stress (PSS) played an important role in symptoms among acculturated subjects, accounting for a significant percentage of the variance in four of the six (66.67%) symptom measures for this group (i.e., Total Symptoms, and Depressive, Obsessive-Compulsive, and Interpersonal Sensitivity symptoms). Appraised generic stress played only a minor role in the symptoms of traditional subjects, however, accounting for a significant percentage of the variance in only two of the six symptom measures. Thus, symptoms among acculturated subjects may be predicted by self-blaming and by ordinary stressors, whereas symptoms among traditional subjects may be predicted by various types of denial of problems.

These differences suggest that acculturation-specific models of African American mental health are needed, along with acculturation-specific therapies that focus on the different, maladaptive coping styles used by some members of both acculturation groups. Further studies with large samples are needed to clarify these preliminary findings, however, in light of the small sample involved; these could highlight the nature of the acculturation-stress-coping-symptom relationship. Such studies are essential because the small sample here necessarily raises questions about the generalizability of these findings. Simultaneously, however, the results were highly significant with this small sample (and so are unlikely to be spurious); this may mean that there are large effects in the population that are worthy of further investigation with large, random samples.

When comparing the findings here to those reported in Chapter 4, we tentatively suggest the following: Physical symptoms and health problems among African Americans (e.g., smoking, hypertension) may be best predicted by racism, with racism predicted by level of acculturation. Psychiatric symptoms among African Americans, on the other hand, may be best predicted by level of acculturation, because acculturation seems to predict coping style used, as well as the relative impact of generic stressors.

NOTES

1. Scores on the PSS were not entered into this general regression model because only 94 of the 153 subjects completed the entire PSS; PSS scores are examined in further analyses here, however.
2. The ns for these analyses vary with the number of subjects who completed the entirety of the instruments entailed.

6

Conclusions and Suggestions for Research

We had three goals in this book. The first was to demonstrate the existence of a coherent, African American culture that persists among African Americans and transcends the enormous social class differences in that population—racist ideology and propaganda to the contrary. We believe that the data in Chapter 3 demonstrate the existence of African American culture and reveal that acculturation is unrelated to social class, education, and the many other status variables that have been used far too often in efforts to deny African American culture.

Our second goal was to investigate the possible role of acculturation in African American physical and mental health. The studies in Chapters 4 and 5 seem to reveal that acculturation may indeed play a role, and thereby suggest that further analysis with large samples is warranted; our goal was not to demonstrate specific, conclusive relationships but to explore possible relationships that could be investigated systematically with large samples. Specifically, the data reported in Chapters 4 and 5 were based on three independent samples of African Americans: Sample 1 consisted of 183 subjects (118 African Americans), Sample 2, of 175 African Americans, and Sample 3, of 153 African Americans. Thus the total number of African Americans to participate in these analyses was 446, a sample from which one cannot possibly generalize to the entire African American population. Likewise, an enormous number of statistical tests were run on these samples to explore various hypotheses and relationships. The results of such analyses thereby cannot be regarded as conclusive and must be understood as limited by the samples involved, as well as by the number of analyses conducted. Thus we neither generalize from these samples to the whole population nor do we present our data as conclusive. Instead, we present the data in Chapters 4 and 5 as exploratory, preliminary analyses of the role of acculturation in African American physical and mental health.

Because they are preliminary, however, does not mean that they are of no value. Instead, these preliminary studies highlight potentially important relationships that require full, systematic investigation and suggest that such investigations will be fruitful. The studies in Chapter 4 *suggest* that racism plays a major role in African American physical health and that it may be mediated by acculturation. Likewise, the studies in Chapter 5 *suggest* that acculturation plays a major role in African American mental health by mediating the impact of generic stressors and of coping styles employed. The purpose of these studies is not to draw conclusions or generalizations but to underscore potential relationships and highlight future, potentially powerful, directions for research. When understood as such, the value of these preliminary studies is clear, and the directions for future research outlined below are then logical, important, and worthy of investigation. Thus, if the data in these preliminary studies have excited readers and have encouraged them to follow up on these investigations (particularly along the lines outlined below) then we met our second goal. We present the African American Acculturation Scale in Appendix B so that others can carry out the investigation begun and suggested here to their logical, empirical ends, and we extend our permission here to others to use the AAAS for research purposes without requesting further permission.

Finally, our third goal was to demolish the belief that African Americans are a race. In Chapter 1, we presented a critical analysis and deconstruction of race, exposing race as little more than political profanity—a four-letter word for a sociopolitical category disguised as a scientific concept. We argued that African Americans must be approached, understood, and treated as an ethnic group (a cultural group) rather than as a race, and we believe that the overwhelming anthropological, historical, and genetic data presented in Chapter 1 support that view. The most compelling evidence for our view that it is culture—not race—that defines African Americans, however, is the preliminary data reported in Chapter 4 on racial discrimination. Again and again in those analyses, we found that racial discrimination against African Americans was not a response to race per se; it was not a response to skin color—to the physical differences that purportedly are the basis for and raison d'être of race. Instead, racial discrimination (i.e., being called a nigger, being discriminated against in housing, health, and employment) was a reaction to level of acculturation: Racism was a negative reaction to African American culture, to African Americans as a cultural group. Such a preliminary finding is consistent with the common claim that dark-skinned African Americans face much discrimination, for we found that they also tend to be traditional and that their traditionality appears to account for that racism. Such findings also are consistent with the historical data presented in Chapter 1, for those data reveal that when race is created, it is a sophisticated sort of slander for a *culture* one views as inferior.

Taken together then, the data in Chapters 1 and 4 suggest that what we have understood to be a reaction to putative race may instead be a reaction to culture and cultural differences today, just as it was in the beginning of the slave trade. What we have regarded as racism may be *cultural racism* for the most part, and this too is worthy of systematic investigation. This, in turn, suggests that racism in our society may not diminish until efforts are made to combat it at the cultural level—at the level where European Americans evaluate African American music as noise; African American interactional styles as histrionic; African American clothing as ostentatious and crass; African American dialect as broken English; African American pronunciations as loose-lipped, sloppy, and slovenly. Yet cultural racism may not be amenable to critique and change until the cultural nature of African Americans is recognized. Thus the need to dismantle and destroy race and races is pressing. So long as a "Black" and (in particular) a "White" race exist, we do not believe that an appreciation of cultural diversity can be achieved. In Appendix A, we outline a few of the steps that psychology can take to dismantle race.

We believe that we have met our three major goals here, and we hope that this work encourages enthusiastic research on the role of acculturation in African American mental and physical health. Some specific studies suggested by these chapters and worthy of attention are outlined below by chapter number.

SUGGESTIONS FOR
FUTURE RESEARCH

Chapter 2. Clearly the most thorough analysis of the acculturative process outlined in Chapter 2 would be a cross-sectional and longitudinal study of the principle of return. In such a study, participants from each of the major developmental time periods (pre-adulthood, early adulthood, middle transition, and late adulthood) would be administered the AAAS and the Schedule of Racist Events repeatedly (every 1 to 5 years) over approximately a 20-year time span. Information regarding such events as the birth of children and/or moving into or out of an ethnic enclave (allopatricity) would be obtained. We would expect that, over time and regardless of the level of acculturation obtained at the first administration of the AAAS, all subjects (particularly those *not* from the late adulthood group) would score as more traditional at the end of the study. The change to being more traditional should be associated with increasing age, a move back into an ethnic enclave, or an increase in the experience of racism. Similarly, the role of ethnic socialization could be tested by a retrospective and prospective study of the messages received about and experiences with European Americans during the childhood of African Americans. Adult African Americans can be asked to recall these experiences, and their responses can be examined for their relationship to level of acculturation. Children (and their parents) can be assessed and then followed for a number of years; the relationships between the ethnic socialization message, the initial prolonged contact, and the level of acculturation (as outlined in Table 2.2) could then be assessed.

Finally, all of the various theories of the processes of acculturation should be tested in combination with other theories regarding the stages of African American development (e.g., Helms's stages of racial identity and the Cross nigrescence model). Simple studies might include administering the RAIS (Helms, 1990) along with the AAAS and assessing the degree to which higher stages of racial identity are associated with being more traditional and lower stages with being more acculturated.

Chapter 3. The AAAS needs to be cross-validated on a large sample of African Americans representing a full array of socioeconomic classes, ages, educational levels, and geographical locations. Although we have conducted one cross-validation study (see Landrine & Klonoff, 1995) and reported it in Chapter 3, our subjects came from the same general geographical area as our original sample. In particular, it would be interesting to compare AAAS scores of African Americans with those of European Americans in the traditionally Southern states. Given the mixing of cultures that occurred during slavery, we would expect that this group of European Americans would score higher on the AAAS than European Americans in other geographical locations but still not as high as African Americans.

Another area of research is apparent from this chapter. This is the development of an acculturation scale that could be used with African American children. Much of the research in both physical and mental health now focuses on factors that put children at risk for negative health behaviors (e.g., smoking, drug use) and poor mental health (e.g., anxiety, depression). Being traditional (and experiencing the racism that appears to be directed toward traditional African Americans) may be a component of risk for African American children. If that is the case, programs that attempt to reduce risk for these children may need to add various strategies for coping with racism to their health and mental health interventions. In addition, the impact of ethnic socialization messages (Chapter 2) on development needs to be assessed with African American children. Until an acculturation scale for African American children has been developed, research on the effects of acculturation on children cannot be undertaken.

Chapter 4. The results from this chapter suggest that traditional African Americans are more likely to smoke and to have high blood pressure and that both of these health problems may be a response to racism (mediated by acculturation). These preliminary findings suggest a number of potentially useful studies. First, although our results were extremely robust (e.g., smokers scored as more traditional in two different samples), the need to replicate these studies on larger samples is clear. Second, the pattern we obtained suggests that traditional African Americans experience higher levels of racism, and this racism is associated with a number of potentially health-damaging behaviors and outcomes. Large-scale studies relating level of acculturation and experienced racism to a wide range of negative health habits (e.g., smoking, drug and alcohol use, eating habits) should be conducted. Initially, these could take the form of surveys in which the AAAS and the Schedule of Racist Events are added to the instruments already in use by the investigator. Third, after our results are replicated on a large scale, intervention studies could then be conducted to evaluate the extent to which culturally sensitive and specific interventions may be more useful for traditional African Americans than the standard interventions developed for (and typically by) the dominant group.

Similar studies looking at the role of acculturation and racism in specific diseases that are known to occur more frequently among African Americans (e.g., hypertension, diabetes; see Klonoff et al., 1995, for a review of the diseases for which African Americans are at risk) should also be undertaken. For example, patients seeking evaluation of their blood pressure or being treated for Type II diabetes could be administered the AAAS and the Schedule of Racist Events as part of their initial evaluation. Scores on these instruments could then be examined for their relationship to measured blood pressure or serum glucose levels. In addition, compliance with medical recommendations (such as lowering the amount of salt in one's diet, losing weight, taking medication as directed, or keeping medical appointments) also can be examined for their relationships both to acculturation and racism. It may be that acculturation (and the racism that may result from being more traditional) accounts for a significant proportion of the variance when African Americans do not comply; if this is demonstrated to be the case, culturally sensitive interventions that take into account level of acculturation could then be developed.

With sufficiently large sample sizes, the types of path analyses described in Chapter 4 can easily be performed. Given that the principle of return hypothesizes that all African Americans will eventually become more traditional, this suggests that, as African Americans age, they will experience increased levels of racism (particularly lifetime racist events, as these accumulate over time), with increased racism having health-deleterious effects. Thus acculturation and racism may help explain differences in death rates between European Americans and African Americans. The role of acculturation and racism in ethnic differences in mortality therefore deserves empirical attention.

Chapter 5. A myriad of studies need to address the role of acculturation and racism in mental health. In the analyses reported here, acculturation accounted for an extremely large proportion of the variance in the report of symptoms—for more variance than any other variable. Additional studies (with large samples) of the impact of level of acculturation on the report of symptoms such as depression and anxiety, using instruments that have been shown to be reliable and valid for African Americans, need to be conducted. Basic information on the role of acculturation in the use of mental health services also needs to be obtained. Although data suggest that African Americans seek mental health services as often as European Americans, they are more likely to discontinue therapy after only one or two sessions (Atkinson, Morten, & Sue, 1983). It may be that level of acculturation is a factor in the decision to terminate therapy and/or that racism is a factor. Mental health services for traditional clients may need to be modified to be more consistent with these clients' cultural beliefs.

In addition, further studies of the role of acculturation in coping strategies need to be conducted. Coping styles defined and categorized by studying European Americans may not adequately reflect the coping strategies used by African Americans. Religious coping, demonstrated to play a positive role in African American physical and mental health (e.g., Neighbors et al., 1983) does not appear to be assessed well by the Ways of Coping, and so this instrument may be inappropriate for African Americans. In addition, level of acculturation may play a significant role in coping because many aspects of being traditional (e.g., reliance on kin networks, the importance of religion) may in and of themselves serve protective functions in ways that are not assessed using the standard measures of coping. Finally, the specific role of racism, particularly as it relates to level of acculturation, needs to be addressed in mental health research. The preliminary data presented here suggest that racism plays a prominent role in physical health and a less prominent role in mental health; by contrast, acculturation may play a prominent role in mental health, and a less prominent one in physical health. These interrelationships merit additional study.

APPENDIX A

Steps Psychologists Can Take to Dismantle Race

There is ample evidence that the time is ripe to unmake America's races. Foremost is the fact that debates about race currently abound in the natural sciences and social sciences and have spilled over into the public consciousness as well. For example, the cover story of *Newsweek* for February 13, 1995, is titled "What color is Black? Science, politics, and racial identity." The articles in that issue detail the deconstruction of race by anthropologists, sociologists, geneticists, and biologists. These deconstructions pick race apart much as we have here (although some of our arguments differ from theirs). New books deconstructing race (e.g., Marks, 1995) should be available about the same time as this one.

In addition, recent debates about the concept of race in psychology similarly suggest that it is time for psychologists to challenge and reject race. For example, in a 1993 paper in the *American Psychologist,* Yee et al. (1993) discussed psychology's use of and problems surrounding the concept of race. The authors carefully documented the objections of other scientists (and of some psychologists) to the prevailing notion of race in the discipline, and they reproduced statements critical of psychology's view of race that have been published by a diversity of professional organizations (e.g., UNESCO). After arguing that the manner in which psychology uses the concept of race violates the ethical principles of the American Psychological Association, Yee et al. suggested that psychology needs "a comprehensive, scientific policy on race to guide research and publications" (p. 1138). This article and the many others by psychologists cited in it are evidence that psychology is ready to tackle race.

Responses to the Yee et al. (1993) article were published in the January 1995 issue of the *American Psychologist.* Two of these (Dole, 1995; Fish, 1995) were in favor of such a policy, with both suggesting that psychology should reject the concept of race. Unfortunately, however, the majority of letters came from those who have made their careers arguing for the scientific (genetic) concept of race (e.g., Jensen, 1995; Rushton, 1995), and so they disagreed with Yee et al. (1993). Nonetheless, the stage has been set for dismantling race.

We believe that psychologists must argue against the use of the concept of race in psychology, for all of the reasons detailed in Chapter 1. Like Yee et al. (1993), we believe that the efforts to dismantle race must be active. Here are some steps that psychologists can take.

1. Divisions of the American Psychological Association (APA) can take a stand on race in their policies and in their journals. Divisions 45, 35, and 9 may need to take the lead.

2. Researchers can cease using the terms *race*, *Blacks*, and *Whites* in their publications and teaching, instead referring to these groups by their specific ethnic group names.

3. Editors of psychological journals can revise their publication policy statements to include the line that the terms *race*, *Black*, and *White* are unscientific and ambiguous and that ethnic groups should be identified accurately.

4. Ethnic-minority psychological associations can and must take a stand on the concept of race, and they can use their power to lobby for changes in the discipline.

Ethnic minority psychologists also can challenge and reject race by ceasing to use racial terms in their research, in the names of their organizations, and in the titles of their journals. Ethnic minority psychologists can also raise the issue in their communities and with the ordinary public and make race a subject of social protest. Race, as we demonstrated, should be open to public as well as scientific criticism, and thus far it has only been vulnerable to the latter because the concept has been disguised as scientific. It may well be time for African Americans to refuse racial classification. It may be time, for example, for the NAACP, the National Urban League, and other African American organizations to reject racial classification.

5. Unlike Yee et al. (1993), we do not believe that a panel is needed to oversee race-IQ studies. Rather, we believe that the Jensens and Rushtons of the nation should be informed that the term *race*, and the use of racial classification schemes, are no longer permitted in psychology because they are unscientific.

Such researchers can and must be permitted to continue their lines of research if we are to remain consistent with the principles of science, academic freedom, and democracy. Such researchers can be required, however, to carefully define their groups in terms of ethnicity. Specifically, Black, White, Latino, Asian, and other groups in such studies must be identified as West Indian or Haitian, Irish or Italian, Mexican or Cuban, Japanese or Chinese.

This demand is fully consistent with the principles of careful scientific research, as well as with the classification of ethnic groups in all other social sciences. These ethnic groups cannot be lumped together into arbitrarily defined races. Race-IQ studies then become ethnicity-IQ studies.

6. Psychologists also can assign the February 13, 1995, issue of *Newsweek* to their classes to facilitate awareness of the tentative status of the concept of race in all other disciplines.

APPENDIX B

Beliefs and Attitudes Survey

Instructions: Please tell us how much you personally agree or disagree with the beliefs and attitudes listed below by circling a number. There is no right or wrong answer. We want your honest opinion.

I Totally Disagree			*I Sort of Agree*			*I Strongly Agree*
Not True At All			*Sort of True*			*Absolutely True*
1	2	3	4	5	6	7

1. One or more of my relatives knows how to do hair.   1 2 3 4 5 6 7
2. When I was young, my parent(s) sent me to stay with a relative (aunt, uncle, grandmother) for a few days or weeks, and then I went back home again.   1 2 3 4 5 6 7

149

| I Totally Disagree | | | I Sort of Agree | | | I Strongly Agree | |
Not True At All			Sort of True			Absolutely True	
1	2	3	4	5	6	7	

3. When I was young, I shared a bed at night with my sister, brother, or some other relative.   1 2 3 4 5 6 7
4. When I was young, my cousin, aunt, grandmother, or other relative lived with me and my family for a while.   1 2 3 4 5 6 7
5. When I was young, my mother or grandmother was the "real" head of the family.   1 2 3 4 5 6 7
6. When I was young, I took a bath with my sister, brother, or some other relative.   1 2 3 4 5 6 7
7. Old people are wise.   1 2 3 4 5 6 7
8. I often lend money or give other types of support to members of my family.   1 2 3 4 5 6 7
9. It's better to try to move your whole family ahead in this world than it is to be out for only yourself.   1 2 3 4 5 6 7
10. A child should not be allowed to call a grown woman by her first name, "Alice." The child should be taught to call her "Miss Alice."   1 2 3 4 5 6 7
11. It's best for infants to sleep with their mothers.   1 2 3 4 5 6 7
12. Some members of my family play the numbers.   1 2 3 4 5 6 7
13. I know how to play bid whist.   1 2 3 4 5 6 7
14. Most of my friends are Black.   1 2 3 4 5 6 7
15. I feel more comfortable around Blacks than around Whites.   1 2 3 4 5 6 7
16. I listen to Black radio stations.   1 2 3 4 5 6 7
17. I try to watch all the Black shows on TV.   1 2 3 4 5 6 7
18. I read (or used to read) *Essence* magazine.   1 2 3 4 5 6 7
19. Most of the music I listen to is by Black artists.   1 2 3 4 5 6 7
20. I like Black music more than White music.   1 2 3 4 5 6 7
21. The person I admire the most is Black.   1 2 3 4 5 6 7
22. When I pass a Black person (a stranger) on the street, I always say hello or nod at them.   1 2 3 4 5 6 7
23. I read (or used to read) *Jet* magazine.   1 2 3 4 5 6 7
24. I usually add salt to my food to make it taste better.   1 2 3 4 5 6 7
25. I know how long you're supposed to cook collard greens.   1 2 3 4 5 6 7
26. I save grease from cooking to use it again later.   1 2 3 4 5 6 7
27. I know how to cook chit'lins.   1 2 3 4 5 6 7
28. I eat grits once in a while.   1 2 3 4 5 6 7
29. I eat a lot of fried food.   1 2 3 4 5 6 7
30. Sometimes I eat collard greens.   1 2 3 4 5 6 7

31. Sometimes I cook ham hocks. 1 2 3 4 5 6 7
32. People say I eat too much salt. 1 2 3 4 5 6 7
33. I eat chit'lins once in a while. 1 2 3 4 5 6 7
34. Most tests (like the SATs and tests to
    get a job) are set up to make sure that Blacks
    don't get high scores on them. 1 2 3 4 5 6 7
35. Deep in their hearts, most White
    people are racists. 1 2 3 4 5 6 7
36. IQ tests were set up purposefully to
    discriminate against Black people. 1 2 3 4 5 6 7
37. Whites don't understand Blacks. 1 2 3 4 5 6 7
38. Some members of my family hate or
    distrust White people. 1 2 3 4 5 6 7
39. I don't trust most White people. 1 2 3 4 5 6 7
40. Most Whites are afraid of Blacks. 1 2 3 4 5 6 7
41. There are many types of blood, such as "high,"
    "low," "thin," and "bad" blood. 1 2 3 4 5 6 7
42. I was taught that you shouldn't take a bath and
    then go outside. 1 2 3 4 5 6 7
43. Illnesses can be classified as natural types
    and unnatural types. 1 2 3 4 5 6 7
44. I believe that some people know how to
    use voodoo. 1 2 3 4 5 6 7
45. Some people in my family use epsom salts. 1 2 3 4 5 6 7
46. I know what "falling out" means. 1 2 3 4 5 6 7
47. Some old Black women/ladies know how to
    cure diseases. 1 2 3 4 5 6 7
48. Some older Black women know a lot about
    pregnancy and childbirth. 1 2 3 4 5 6 7
49. Prayer can cure disease. 1 2 3 4 5 6 7
50. I have seen people "fall out." 1 2 3 4 5 6 7
51. If doctors can't cure you, you should try going
    to a root doctor or to your minister. 1 2 3 4 5 6 7
52. I have "fallen out." 1 2 3 4 5 6 7
53. I believe in heaven and hell. 1 2 3 4 5 6 7
54. I like gospel music. 1 2 3 4 5 6 7
55. The church is the heart of the Black community. 1 2 3 4 5 6 7
56. I am currently a member of a Black church. 1 2 3 4 5 6 7
57. I have seen people "get the spirit" or speak
    in tongues. 1 2 3 4 5 6 7
58. I believe in the Holy Ghost. 1 2 3 4 5 6 7
59. I went to a mostly Black elementary school. 1 2 3 4 5 6 7
60. When I was young, I was a member of a
    Black church. 1 2 3 4 5 6 7
61. I grew up in a mostly Black neighborhood. 1 2 3 4 5 6 7
62. The biggest insult is an insult to your mother. 1 2 3 4 5 6 7
63. I went to (or go to) a mostly Black high school. 1 2 3 4 5 6 7

64. Dancing was an important part of my childhood.   1 2 3 4 5 6 7
65. I used to sing in the church choir.   1 2 3 4 5 6 7
66. When I was a child, I used to play tonk.   1 2 3 4 5 6 7
67. When I was young, I used to jump double-dutch.   1 2 3 4 5 6 7
68. I currently live in a mostly Black neighborhood.   1 2 3 4 5 6 7
69. I used to like to watch *Soul Train*.   1 2 3 4 5 6 7
70. What goes around, comes around.   1 2 3 4 5 6 7
71. There's some truth to many old superstitions.   1 2 3 4 5 6 7
72. I avoid splitting a pole.   1 2 3 4 5 6 7
73. When the palm of your hand itches, you'll
receive some money.   1 2 3 4 5 6 7
74. I eat black-eyed peas on New Year's Eve.   1 2 3 4 5 6 7

SCORING THE AAAS

ITEM SCORES

A subject's score on each item is the number s/he circled for that item. The range of these scores is 1 to 7.

SUBSCALE SCORES

Scores on the subscales should be computed as follows:
Traditional Family Practices and Values: Σ of the scores on Items 1 to 12
Preference for African American Things: Σ of the scores on Items 13 to 23
Traditional Foods: Σ of the scores on Items 24 to 33
Interracial Attitudes: Σ of the scores on Items 34 to 40
Traditional Health Beliefs and Practices: Σ of the scores on Items 41 to 52
Religious Beliefs and Practices: Σ of the scores on Items 53 to 58
Traditional Socialization: Σ of the scores on Items 59 to 69
Superstitions: Σ of the scores on Items 70 to 74

AAAS TOTAL SCORE

Each subject's Total Score = Σ of the scores on each subscale (i.e., Σ of the scores on all 74 items).

MISSING VALUES

Subjects must be encouraged to complete all items. If a subject omits an item, (a) sum the scores on the items completed for the subscale in question; (b) divide this total by the number of items completed in the subscale; (c) use this individual subscale mean as the subject's score on the missing item. Example: A subject skips one of the six items that constitute the Attitudes subscale but answered all of the others by circling 5, 5, 5, 5, 7. Sum his/her scores on the five items s/he completed (Σ of $5 + 5 + 5 + 5 + 7 = 27$) and divide this by the number of completed items (5). The result ($27 \div 5 = 5.4$) can be used as the subject's score on the missing item.

References

Abrahams, R. D. (1970). *Positively Black*. Englewood Cliffs, NJ: Prentice Hall.

American Cancer Society. (1989). *Cancer facts and figures, 1989*. Atlanta, GA: Author.

Aries, P. (1962). *Centuries of childhood*. New York: Vintage.

Asante, M. K. (1988). *Afrocentricity*. Trenton, NJ: Africa World Press.

Atkinson, D. R., Morten, G., & Sue, D. W. (1983). *Counseling American minorities*. Dubuque, IA: William C. Brown.

Baer, H. (1985). Toward a systematic typology of Black folk healers. *Phylon, 43*, 327-343.

Bailey, E. J. (1987). Sociocultural factors and health care seeking among Black Americans. *Journal of the National Medical Association, 79*, 389-392.

Bailey, E. J. (1991). *Urban African-American health care*. New York: University Press of America.

Baldwin, J. A. (1981). Notes on an Africentric theory of Black personality testing. *Western Journal of Black Studies, 5*, 172-179.

Barnes, A. (1981). The Black kinship system. *Phylon, 42*, 369-380.

Basso, K., & Selby, H. (1976). *Meaning in anthropology*. Albuquerque: University of New Mexico.

Benedict, R. (1950). *Patterns of culture*. New York: New American Library.

154

Berry, J. W., Kalin, R., & Taylor, D. M. (1977). *Multiculturalism and ethnic attitudes in Canada*. Ottawa: Minister of Supply and Services.

Botvin, G., & Eng, A. (1980). A comprehensive school-based smoking prevention program. *Journal of School Health, 11,* 209-213.

Boyd-Franklin, N. (1989a). *Black families in therapy*. New York: Guilford.

Boyd-Franklin, N. (1989b). Racism, racial identification, and skin color issues. In N. Boyd-Franklin, *Black families in therapy* (pp. 25-41). New York: Guilford.

Bransford, J. D., & McCarrell, N. S. (1977). A sketch of a cognitive approach to comprehension. In P. N. Johnson-Laird & P. C. Wason (Eds.), *Thinking: Readings in cognitive science* (p. 377). New York: Cambridge University Press.

Breslau, N., Kilbey, M. M., & Andreski, P. (1991). Nicotine dependence, major depression, and anxiety in young adults. *Archives of General Psychiatry, 48*(12), 1069-1074.

Breton, R. (1978). Stratification and conflict between ethnolinguistic communities with different social structures. *Canadian Review of Sociology and Anthropology, 15,* 148-157.

Brimelow, P. (1995). *Alien nation*. New York: Random House.

Brown, D. R., & Gary, L. E. (1987). Stressful life events, social support networks, and the physical and mental health of urban Black adults. *Journal of Human Stress, 13,* 165-174.

Bruner, J. S. (1957). Going beyond information given. In *Contemporary approaches to cognition: A symposium held at the University of Colorado* (p. 473). Cambridge, MA: Harvard University Press.

Burnam, M. A., Hough, R. L., Karno, M., Escobar, J. I., & Telles, C. A. (1987). Acculturation and lifetime prevalence of psychiatric disorders among Mexican Americans in Los Angeles. *Journal of Health and Social Behavior, 28,* 89-102.

Carter, R. T., & Helms, J. E. (1987, January). The relationship of Black value-orientations to racial identity attitudes. *Measurement and Evaluation in Counseling and Development,* pp. 185-195.

Caudill, W., & Plath, D. (1966). Who sleeps by whom? Parent-child involvement in urban Japanese families. *Psychiatry, 29,* 344-366.

Centers for Disease Control. (1989). *Surgeon General's report on smoking*. Washington, DC: Central Office for Health Promotion and Education on Smoking and Health, Government Printing Office.

Chunn, J., Dunston, P., & Ross-Sheriff, F. (1983). *Mental health and people of color*. Washington, DC: Howard University Press.

Clark, D. (1992). Irish Americans. In J. D. Buenker & L. A. Ratner (Eds.), *Multiculturalism in the United States: A comparative guide to acculturation and ethnicity* (pp. 77-102). New York: Greenwood.

Cohen, A. (1969). *Custom and politics in urban Africa*. Berkeley: University of California Press.

Cohen, S. (1986). Contrasting the Hassles scale and the Perceived Stress Scale: Who's really measuring appraised stress? *American Psychologist, 41,* 716-718.

Cohen, S., Kamarck, T., & Mermelstein, R. (1983). A global measure of perceived stress. *Journal of Health and Social Behavior, 24,* 385-396.

Cose, E. (1993). *The rage of the privileged class.* New York: Harper Collins.

Crowell, J., Keener, M., Ginsburg, N., & Anders, T. (1987). Sleep habits in toddlers 18 to 36 months old. *American Journal of Child and Adolescent Psychiatry, 26,* 510-515.

Crowley, D. (1977). *African folklore in the new world.* Austin: University of Texas Press.

Cuellar, I., Harris, I. C., & Jasso, R. (1980). An acculturation scale for Mexican-American normal and clinical populations. *Hispanic Journal of Behavioral Science, 2,* 199-217.

Dana, R. (1993). *Multicultural assessment perspectives for professional psychology.* Needham Heights, MA: Allyn/Bacon.

D'Andrade, R. (1981). The cultural part of cognition. *Cognitive Science, 5,* 179-195.

Davis, F. J. (1991). *Who is Black? One nation's definition.* State College: Pennsylvania State University Press.

Davis, R. M. (1987). Current trends in cigarette advertising and marketing. *New England Journal of Medicine, 316,* 725-732.

Deloria, V., Jr. (1983). Indians today, the real and the unreal. In D. R. Atkinson, G. Morten, & D. W. Sue (Eds.), *Counseling American minorities: A cross-cultural perspective* (pp. 47-76). Dubuque, IA: William C. Brown.

Dembo, D. H., & Hughes, M. (1990). Socialization and racial identity among Black Americans. *Social Psychology Quarterly, 53,* 364-374.

Derogatis, L. R., Lipman, R. S., Rickles, K., Uhlenhuth, E. H., & Covi, L. (1974). The Hopkins Symptom Checklist (HSCL): A self-report symptom inventory. *Behavioral Science, 19,* 1-15.

Dohrenwend, B. S., & Dohrenwend, B. P. (1970). Class and race as status-related sources of stress. In S. Levine & N. A. Scotch (Eds.), *Social stress* (pp. 111-140). Chicago: Aldine.

Dohrenwend, B. S., & Dohrenwend, B. P. (1981). *Stressful life events and their contexts.* New York: Prodist.

Dohrenwend, B. S., Krasnoff, L., Askenasy, A. R., & Dohrenwend, B. P. (1978). Exemplification of a method for scaling life events; The PERI-Life Events Scale. *Journal of Health and Social Behavior, 19,* 205-229.

Dole, A. A. (1995). Why not drop "race" as a term? *American Psychologist, 50*(1), 40.

Dressler, W. W. (1980). Coping dispositions, social supports, and health status. *Ethos, 8,* 146-171.

Dressler, W. W. (1982). *Hypertension and culture change: Acculturation and disease in the West Indies.* New York: Redgrave.

Dressler, W. W. (1985a). Extended family relationships, social support, and mental health in a southern Black community. *Journal of Health and Social Behavior, 26,* 39-48.

Dressler, W. W. (1985b). The social and cultural context of coping. *Social Science and Medicine, 21,* 499-506.

Dressler, W. W. (1986). Unemployment and depressive symptoms in southern Black community. *Journal of Nervous and Mental Disease, 174,* 639-645.

Dressler, W. W., Mata, A., Chavez, A., & Viteri, F. E. (1987). Arterial blood pressure and modernization in a Mexican community. *Social Science and Medicine, 24,* 679-687.

DuBois, W. E. B. (1961). *The souls of Black folks.* New York: Fawcett.

Ellinson, C. G. (1990). Family ties, friendships, and subjective well-being among Black Americans. *Journal of Marriage and the Family, 52,* 298-310.

Enloe, C. (1980). *Ethnic soldiers.* GA: University of Georgia Press.

Epperson, T. W. (1994). The politics of empiricism and the construction of race as an analytical category. *Transforming Anthropology, 5,* 15-19.

Esman, M. J. (1987). Politics and economic power. *Comparative Politics, 19,* 395-417.

Fairchild, H. H., Yee, A. H., Wyatt, G. E., & Weizmann, F. M. (1995). Readdressing psychology's problems with race. *American Psychologist, 50,* 46-47.

Farber, B., Mindel, C. H., & Lazerwitz, B. (1981). The Jewish American family. In C. H. Mindel & R. W. Haberstein (Eds.), *Ethnic families in America* (pp. 350-385). New York: Elsevier.

Feagin, J., & Feagin, C. (1978). *Discrimination American style: Institutional racism and sexism.* Englewood Cliffs, NJ: Prentice Hall.

Festinger, L. (1954). A theory of social comparison processes. *Human Relations, 2,* 117-140.

Fish, J. M. (1995). Why psychologists should learn some anthropology. *American Psychologist, 50*(1), 44-45.

Fish, S. (1979). Normal circumstances, literal language, direct speech acts, the ordinary, the obvious, what goes without saying, and other special cases. In P. Rabinow & W. M. Sullivan (Eds.), *Interpretive social science* (pp. 243-265). Berkeley: University of California Press.

Fleming, R., Leventhal, H., Glynn, K., & Ershler, J. (1989). The role of cigarettes in the initiation and early progression of substance use. *Addictive Behavior, 14,* 261-272.

Folkman, S., Lazarus, R. S., Dunkel-Schetter, C., DeLongis, A., & Gruen, R. J. (1986). Dynamics of a stressful encounter: Cognitive appraisal, coping, and encounter outcomes. *Journal of Personality and Social Psychology, 50,* 993-1003.

Frazier, E. F. (1963). *The Negro church in America.* New York: Schocken.

Friendberg, E. (1965). *Coming of age in America.* New York: Random House.

Gailey, C. W. (1994). Politics, colonialism, and the mutable color of southern Pacific peoples. *Transforming Anthropology, 5,* 34-40.

Genovese, E. (1974). *Roll Jordan, roll.* New York: Pantheon.

Gentry, W. D., Chesney, A. P., Gary, H. E., Hall, R. P., & Harburg, E. (1982). Habitual anger-coping style: I. Affect on mean blood pressure and risk for essential hypertension. *Psychosomatic Medicine, 44,* 195-202.

Geoghegan, W. (1971). Information processing systems in culture. In P. Kay (Ed.), *Explorations in mathematical anthropology.* Cambridge: MIT Press.

Giffith, J. (1985). Social support providers: Who are they? *Basic and Applied Social Psychology, 6*(1), 41-60.

Gillis, J. R. (1981). *Youth and history*. New York: Academic Press.

Goodson, M. (1987). Medical-botanical contributions of African slave women to American medicine. *The Western Journal of Black Studies, 2,* 198-203.

Gordon, M. M. (1964). *Assimilation in American life.* New York: Oxford University Press.

Gordon, M. M. (1978). *Human nature, class, and ethnicity.* New York: Oxford University Press.

Gossett, T. F. (1965). *Race: The history of an idea in America.* New York: Schocken.

Gottlieb, N. H., & Green, L. W. (1987). Ethnicity and lifestyle risk. *American Journal of Health Promotion, 2*(1), 37-45.

Gould, S. J. (1977). *Ever since Darwin: Reflections in natural history.* New York: Norton.

Gould, S. J. (1981). *The mismeasure of man.* New York: Norton.

Gran, P. (1994). Race and racism in the modern world: How it works in different hegemonies. *Transforming Anthropology, 5,* 8-14.

Greenberg, L. (1944). *The Jews in Russia.* New Haven, CT: Yale University Press.

Gregory, R. L. (1970). *The intelligent eye.* London: Weidenfeld & Nicolson.

Guttman, H. G. (1974). *The Black family in slavery and freedom.* New York: Pantheon.

Hall, A. L., & Bourne, P. G. (1973). Indigenous therapists in a Black urban community. *Archives of General Psychiatry, 28,* 137-142.

Harburg, E., Erfurt, J. C., Havenstein, L. S., Chape, C., Schull, W. J., & Schork, M. A. (1973). Socio-ecological stress, suppressed hostility, skin color, and black-white male blood pressure. *Psychosomatic Medicine, 35,* 276-296.

Harris, M. (1964). *Patterns of race in the Americas.* New York: Walker.

Harrison, A. O., Wilson, M. N., Pine, C. J., Chan, S. Q., & Buriel, R. (1990). Family ecologies of ethnic minority children. *Child Development, 61,* 347-362.

Harrison, F. (1994). Racial and gender inequalities in health and health care. *Medical Anthropology Quarterly, 8*(1), 90-95.

Hays, W. (1973). Extended kinship relations in Black and White families. *Journal of Marriage and the Family, 35,* 51-57.

Hays, W. L. (1981). *Statistics.* New York: Holt, Rinehart, & Winston.

Hellie, R. (1982). *Slavery in Russia.* Chicago: University of Chicago Press.

Helmholtz, H. (1962). *Treatise on physiological optics, III* (J. P. C. Southall, Ed.). New York: Dover. (Original work published 1866)

Helms, J. E. (1990). *Black and White racial identity.* New York: Greenwood.

Herrnstein, R. J., & Murray, C. (1994). *The bell curve: Intelligence and class structure in American life.* New York: Free Press.

Hersvokits, M. J. (1941). *The myth of the Negro past.* New York: Harper.

Hildreth, C. J., & Saunders, E. (1992). Heart disease, stroke, and hypertension in Blacks. In R. L. Braithwaite & S. E. Taylor (Eds.), *Health issues in the Black community* (pp. 90-105). San Francisco: Jossey-Bass.

Hill, C. E. (1973). Black healing practices in the rural south. *Journal of Popular Culture, 6,* 829-853.

Hill, C. E. (1976). Folk medical belief system in the American South. *Southern Medicine,* 11-17.

Hill, R. (1977). *Informal adoption among Black families.* Washington, DC: Urban League Research Department.

Hoffman, T., Dana, R. H., & Bolton, B. (1985). Measured acculturation and MMPI-168 performance of Native American adults. *Journal of Cross-Cultural Psychology, 16,* 243-256.

hooks, b. (1992). Eating the other. In b. hooks, *Black looks: Race and representation* (pp. 21-39). Boston: South End Press.

Idson, T., & Price, H. (1992). An analysis of wage differentials by gender and ethnicity in the public sector. *The Review of Black Political Economy, 20,* 75-97.

Jackson, J. J. (1981). Urban Black Americans. In A. Harwood (Ed.), *Ethnicity and medical care* (pp. 37-129). Cambridge: MIT Press.

James, S. A. (1987). Psychosocial precursors of hypertension: A review of the epidemiological evidence. *Circulation, 76*(Supplement I), 160-166.

Jensen, A. R. (1995). Psychological research on race differences. *American Psychologist, 50*(1), 41-42.

Jensen, A. R., & Johnson, F. W. (1994). Race and sex differences in head size and IQ. *Intelligence, 18,* 309-333.

Jones, E., & Korchin, S. J. (1982). *Minority mental health.* New York: Praeger.

Jones, J. M. (1986). Racism: A cultural analysis of the problem. In J. F. Dovidio & S. Gaertner (Eds.), *Prejudice, discrimination, and racism.* Orlando, FL: Academic Press.

Jones, J. M. (1991a). The politics of personality: Being Black in America. In R. L. Jones (Ed.), *Black psychology* (pp. 305-318). Hampton, VA: Cobb & Henry.

Jones, J. M. (1991b). Psychological models of race: What have they been and what should they be? In J. D. Goodchilds (Ed.), *Psychological perspectives on human diversity in America* (pp. 7-46). Washington DC: American Psychological Association.

Jordan, W. (1975). Voodoo medicine. In R. Williams (Ed.), *Textbook of Black-related diseases* (pp. 716-738). New York: McGraw-Hill.

Jordan, W. (1979). The roots and practice of Voodoo medicine. *Urban Health, 8,* 38-41.

Kambon, K. K. K. (1992). *The African personality in America.* Tallahassee, FL: Nubian Nation.

Kamin, L. J. (1974). *The science and politics of IQ.* Potomac, MD: Lawrence Erlbaum.

Kanner, A. D., Coyne, J. C., Schaeffer, C., & Lazarus, R. S. (1981). Comparison of two modes of stress measurement: Daily hassles and uplifts versus major life events. *Journal of Behavioral Medicine, 4,* 1-39.

Kantowitz, E. R. (1992). Polish Americans. In J. D. Buenker & L. A. Ratner (Eds.), *Multiculturalism in the United States: A comparative guide to acculturation and ethnicity* (pp. 131-148). New York: Greenwood.

Kessen, W. (1979). The American child and other cultural inventions. *American Psychologist, 34,* 815-820.

Kett, J. F. (1976). *Rite of passage.* New York: Basic Books.

Klonoff, E. A., Landrine, H., & Scott, J. (1995). Double jeopardy: Ethnicity and gender in research. In H. Landrine (Ed.), *Bringing cultural diversity to feminist psychology: Theory, research, and practice* (pp. 335-380). Washington, DC: American Psychological Association.

Kourvetaris, G. A. (1981). The Greek American family. In C. H. Mindel & R. W. Haberstein (Eds.), *Ethnic families in America* (pp. 163-188). New York: Elsevier.

Krieger, N. (1990). Racial and gender discrimination: Risk factors for high blood pressure? *Social Science and Medicine, 30,* 1273-1281.

LaFromboise, T., Coleman, H., & Gerton, J. (1993). Psychological impact of biculturalism. *Psychological Bulletin, 114*(3), 395-412.

Lambert, W. E., Mermigis, L., & Taylor, D. M. (1986). Greek Canadians' attitudes toward own group and other Canadian ethnic groups: A test of the multiculturalism hypothesis. *The Canadian Journal of Behavioral Sciences, 18,* 35-51.

Lambert, W. E., & Taylor, D. M. (1990). *Coping with cultural and racial diversity in urban America.* New York: Praeger.

Landrine, H. (1992). Clinical implications of cultural differences. *Clinical Psychology Review, 12,* 401-415.

Landrine, H., & Klonoff, E. A. (1992). Culture and health-related schema: Review and proposal for interdisciplinary integration. *Health Psychology, 11,* 267-276.

Landrine, H., & Klonoff, E. A. (1994). Cultural diversity in causal attributions for illness. *Journal of Behavioral Medicine, 17,* 181-193.

Landrine, H., & Klonoff, E. A. (1995). The African-American Acculturation Scale II: Cross-validation and short form. *Journal of Black Psychology, 21,* 124-152.

Landrine, H., & Klonoff, E. A. (1996). The Schedule of Racist Events: A measure of racial discrimination and a study of its negative physical and mental consequences. *Journal of Black Psychology,* in press.

Landrine, H., Klonoff, E. A., Alcaraz, R., Scott, J., & Wilkins, J. (1995). Multiple variables in discrimination. In B. Lott & D. Maluso (Eds.), *The social psychology of interpersonal discrimination.* New York: Guilford.

Landrine, H., Klonoff, E. A., & Brown-Collins, A. (1992). Cultural diversity and methodology in feminist psychology. *Psychology of Women Quarterly, 16,* 145-163.

Landrine, H., Klonoff, E. A., & Fritz, J. M. (1994). Preventing cigarette sales to minors: The need for contextual, sociocultural analyses. *Preventive Medicine, 23,* 322-327.

Landrine, H., Klonoff, E. A., & Richardson, J. L. (1993). *Cultural diversity in the predictors of adolescent substance use.* Paper presented at the annual meeting of the Association for Advancement of Behavior Therapy, Atlanta, GA.

Landrine, H., Richardson, J. L., Klonoff, E. A., & Flay, B. (1994). Cultural diversity in the predictors of adolescent cigarette smoking. *Journal of Behavioral Medicine, 17*(3) 331-346.

Lazarus, R. S. (1966). *Psychological stress and the coping process.* New York: McGraw-Hill.

Lazarus, R. S., DeLongis, A., Folkman, S., & Gruen, R. (1985). Stress and adaptational outcomes: The problem of confounded measures. *American Psychologist, 40,* 770-779.

Lazarus, R. S., & Folkman, S. (1984). *Stress, appraisal, and coping.* New York: Springer.

Lazarus, R. S., & Folkman, S. (1986). Reply to Cohen. *American Psychologist, 41,* 718-719.

Lazarus, R. S., & Launier, R. (1978). Stress-related transactions between person and environment. In L. A. Pervin & M. Lewis (Eds.), *Perspectives in interactional psychology* (pp. 287-327). New York: Plenum.

Levine, L. (1977). *Black culture and Black consciousness.* New York: Oxford University Press.

Lewis, B. (1990). *Race and slavery in the Middle East.* New York: Oxford University Press.

Lewotin, R., Rose, S., & Kamin, G. (1984). *Not in our genes: Biology, ideology, and human nature.* New York: Pantheon.

Littlefield, A., Liebermann, L., & Reynolds, L. T. (1982). Redefining race: The potential demise of a concept in physical anthropology. *Current Anthropology, 23,* 641-655.

Lozoff, B., Wolf, A., & Davis, N. (1984). Co-sleeping in urban families with young children in the United States. *Pediatrics, 74,* 171-182.

Magubane, B. M. (1987). *The ties that bind: African-American consciousness of Africa.* Trenton, NJ: Africa World Press.

Mandansky, D., & Edelbrock, C. (1990). Co-sleeping in a community sample of 2- and 3-year-old children. *Pediatrics, 86,* 197-280.

Marín, G., Marín, B. V., Otero-Sabogal, R., Sabogal, F., & Perez-Stable, E. J. (1989). The role of acculturation in the attitudes, norms, and expectancies of Hispanic smokers. *Journal of Cross-Cultural Psychology, 20*(4), 399-415.

Maín, G., Perez-Stable, E. J., & Marín, B. V. (1989). Cigarette smoking among San Francisco Hispanics. *American Journal of Public Health, 79,* 196-198.

Markides, K. S., Coreil, J., & Ray, L. A. (1987). Smoking among Mexican Americans. *American Journal of Public Health, 77,* 708-711.

Marks, J. (1995). *Human biodiversity.* New York: deGruyter.

Marmot, M. G., & Syme, S. L. (1976). Acculturation and coronary heart disease in Japanese-Americans. *American Journal of Epidemiology, 104,* 225-247.

Martin, R. V., Cummings, S. R., & Coates, T. J. (1990). Ethnicity and smoking: Differences in White, Black, and Asian medical patients who smoke. *American Journal of Preventive Medicine, 6,* 194-199.

Martinez, J. L., & Mendoza, R. H. (1984). *Chicano psychology.* Orlando, FL: Academic Press.

Masuda, M., Matsumoto, G. H., & Meredith, G. M. (1970). Ethnic identity in three generations of Japanese Americans. *Journal of Social Psychology, 81,* 199-207.

Mbiti, J.S. (1975). *African religions and philosophies.* Garden City, NY: Anchor.

McAdoo, H. P. (1981). *Black families.* Beverly Hills, CA: Sage.

McArthur, L. Z., & Baron, R. M. (1983). Toward an ecological theory of social perception. *Psychological Review, 90,* 215-238.

Mendoza, R. H. (1989). An empirical scale to measure type and degree of acculturation in Mexican American adolescents and adults. *Journal of Cross-Cultural Psychology, 20,* 372-385.

Miller, G. A. (1977). Practical and lexical knowledge. In P. N. Johnson-Laird & P. C. Wason, *Thinking* (p. 400). New York: Cambridge University Press.

Montagu, A. (1945). *Man's most dangerous myth: The fallacy of race.* New York: Columbia University Press.

Montagu, A. (1962). The concept of race. *American Anthropologist, 64,* 919-928.

Montgomery, G. T., & Orozco, S. (1985). Mexican Americans' performance on the MMPI as a function of level of acculturation. *Journal of Clinical Psychology, 41,* 203-212.

Morelli, G., Rogoff, B., Oppenheim, D., & Goldsmith, D. (1992). Cultural variation in infants' sleeping arrangements. *Developmental Psychology, 28,* 604-613.

Moss, L., & Cappannari, S. (1960). Folklore and medicine in an Italian village. *Journal of American Folklore, 63,* 95-102.

Myers, L. J. (1988). *Understanding an Afrocentric world view.* Dubuque, IA: Kendall/Hunt.

Myrdal, G. (1944). *An American dilemma.* New York: Harper.

Nagel, J. (1982). The political mobilization of Native Americans. *Social Science Journal, 19,* 37-46.

Nagel, J., & Olzak, S. (1982). Ethnic mobilization in new and old states. *Social Problems, 30,* 127-143.

National Institute of Mental Health. (1983). *Research highlights: Extramural research.* Washington, DC: Government Printing Office.

Neal, A. M., & Wilson, M. L. (1989). The role of skin color and features in the Black community. *Clinical Psychology Review, 9,* 323-333.

Neff, J. A., & Husaini, B. A. (1980). Race, socioeconomic status, and psychiatric impairment. *Journal of Community Psychology, 8,* 16-19.

Neighbors, H. W., Jackson, J. S., & Bowman, P. J. (1983). Stress, coping, and Black mental health: Preliminary findings from a national study. *Prevention in Human Services, 2*(3), 5-29.

Neilsen, F. (1986). The Flemish movement in Belgium after World War II. *American Sociological Review, 45,* 76-94.

Nobles, W. (1980). African philosophy: Foundations for Black psychology. In R. Jones (Ed.), *Black psychology* (pp. 23-36). New York: Harper & Row.

Nobles, W. W. (1986). *African psychology.* Oakland, CA: Black Family Institute.

Novak, M. (1972). *The rise of the unmeltable ethnics.* New York: Macmillan.

Oetting, E. R., & Beauvais, F. (1990-1991). Orthogonal cultural identification theory: The cultural identification of minority adolescents. *International Journal of the Addictions, 25,* 655-685.

Oetting, E. R., Edwards, R. W., & Beauvais, F. (1989). Drugs and Native-American youth. In B. Segal (Ed.), *Perspectives on adolescent drug use* (pp. 1-34). New York: Harworth.

Okazawa-Rey, M., Robinson, T. L., & Ward, J. V. (1987). Black women and the politics of skin color and hair. *Women and Therapy, 6,* 89-102.

Olzak, S. (1982). Ethnic mobilization in Quebec. *Ethnic and Racial Studies, 5,* 253-275.

Padilla, A. (1980). *Acculturation.* Boulder, CO: Westview.

Peters, M. F. (1985). Racial socialization of young Black children. In H. P. McAdoo & J. L. McAdoo (Eds.), *Black children* (pp. 159-173). Beverly Hills, CA: Sage.

Pipes, W. H. (1981). Old-time religion. In H. McAdoo (Ed.), *Black families* (pp. 54-76). Beverly Hills, CA: Sage.

Polednak, A. P. (1989). *Racial and ethnic differences in disease.* New York: Oxford University Press.

Portes, A. (1984). The rise of ethnicity. *American Sociological Review, 49,* 383-397.

Postigilone, G. A. (1983). *Ethnicity and American social theory: Toward critical pluralism.* New York: University Press of America.

Quadagno, J. S. (1981). The Italian American family. In C. H. Mindel & R. W. Haberstein (Eds.), *Ethnic families in America* (pp. 61-85). New York: Elsevier.

Quigley, H., & Glock, C.(1979). *Antisemitism in America.* New York: Free Press.

Robinson, T. L., & Ward, J. V. (1995). African-American adolescents and skin color. *Journal of Black Psychology, 21*(3), 256-274.

Rushton, J. P. (1992). Cranial capacity related to sex, rank, and race. *Intelligence, 16,* 401-413.

Rushton, J. P. (1994). Sex and race differences in cranial capacity from International Labour Office data. *Intelligence, 19,* 281-294.

Rushton, J. P. (1995). Construct validity, censorship, and the genetics of race. *American Psychologist, 50*(1), 40-41.

Schaar, H. M. (1958). *The course of modern Jewish history.* New York: World.

Scott, C. (1974). Health and healing practices among five ethnic groups in Miami, Florida. *Public Health Reports, 89* (6), 524-532.

Shapiro, E. (1992). Jewish-Americans. In J. D. Buenker & L. A. Ratner (Eds.), *Multiculturalism in the United States: A comparative guide to acculturation and ethnicity* (pp. 149-172). New York: Greenwood.

Shimkin, D., Shimkin, E., & Frate, D. (1978). *The extended family in Black societies.* Paris: Mouton.

Shore, B. (1991). Twice born, once conceived: Meaning construction and cultural cognition. *American Anthropologist, 93,* 9-27.

Shweder, R., & LeVine, R. A. (1984). *Culture theory.* Cambridge, UK: Cambridge University Press.

Sinkler, G. (1972). *Racial attitudes of American presidents from Abraham Lincoln to Theodore Roosevelt.* New York: Doubleday/Anchor.

Smith, K., McGraw, S. A., & Carrillo, J. E. (1991). Factors affecting cigarette smoking and intention to smoke among Puerto Rican-American high school students. *Hispanic Journal of Behavioral Sciences, 13*(4), 401-411.

Snow, L. F. (1974). Folk medical beliefs and their implications for the care of patients. *Annals of Internal Medicine, 81,* 82-96.

Snow, L. F. (1977). Popular medicine in a Black neighborhood. In E. H. Spicer (Ed.), *Ethnic medicine in the Southwest* (pp. 19-95). Tucson: University of Arizona Press.

Snow, L. F. (1978). Sorcerers, saints, and charlatans: Black folk healers in urban America. *Culture, Medicine, and Psychiatry, 2,* 69-106.

Sommers-Flanagan, J., & Greenberg, R. P. (1989). Psychosocial variables and hypertension: A new look at an old controversy. *Journal of Nervous and Mental Disease, 177,* 15-24.

Sowell, T. (1978a). *American ethnic groups.* New York: Urban Institute.

Sowell, T. (1978b). Three Black histories. In T. Sowell (Ed.), *American ethnic groups* (pp. 7-64). New York: Urban Institute.

Sowell, T. (1994). *Race and culture: A world view.* New York: Basic Books.

Stack, C. (1974). *All our kin.* New York: Harper & Row.

Stanton, W. (1960). *The leopard's spots: Scientific attitudes towards race in American 1815-1859.* Chicago: University of Chicago Press.

Stillman, F. A., Bone, L. R., & Rand, C. (1993). Heart, body and soul: A church-based smoking cessation program for urban African-Americans. *Preventive Medicine, 22*(3), 335.

Szapocznik, J., & Kurtines, W. (1980). Acculturation, biculturalism, and adjustment among Cuban Americans. In A. M. Padilla (Ed.), *Acculturation: Theory, models, and some new findings* (pp. 139-159). Boulder, CO: Westview.

Szapocznik, J., Scopetta, M. A., & Kurtines, W. (1978). Theory and measurement of acculturation. *Interamerican Journal of Psychology, 12,* 113-130.

Taylor, S. (1991). *Health psychology.* New York: McGraw-Hill.

Terrell, F., & Terrell, S. L. (1981). An inventory to measure cultural mistrust among Blacks. *Western Journal of Black Studies, 5,* 180-184.

Thompson, V. L. S. (1994). Socialization to race and its relationship to racial identification among African-Americans. *Journal of Black Psychology, 20* 175-188.

U.S. Bureau of the Census (1989). Projections of the population of the United States. In *Current population reports* (Series P-25, No. 1018). Washington, DC: Government Printing Office.

U.S. Department of Health, Education, and Welfare. (1979). *Healthy people: A report of the Surgeon General on health promotion and disease prevention* (USPHS Publication No. 79-55071). Washington, DC: Government Printing Office.

van den Berghe, P. L. (1978). *Race and racism: A comparative approach.* New York: John Wiley.

Vogel, F., & Motulsky, A. G. (1986). *Human genetics.* Berlin: Springer-Verlag.

Ward, M.C. (1971). *Them children.* New York: Holt, Rinehart, & Winston.

Weidman, H. H. (1979). Falling-out. *Social Science and Medicine, 13B,* 95-112.

Westermann, W. L. (1955). *The slave systems of Greek and Roman antiquity.* Philadelphia: American Philosophical Society.

Weston, R. F. (1972). *Racism in U.S. imperialism: The influence of racial assumptions on American foreign policy 1893-1946.* Columbia: University of South Carolina Press.

Whiting, B. B., & Edwards, C. (1988). *Children of different worlds.* Cambridge, MA: Harvard University Press.

Wilson, W. (1980). *The declining significance of race.* Chicago: University of Chicago Press.

Yao, E. L. (1979). The assimilation of contemporary Chinese immigrants. *Journal of Psychology, 101,* 107-113.

Yee, A. H., Fairchild, H. H., Weizmann, F., & Wyatt, G. E. (1993). Addressing psychology's problems with race. *American Psychologist, 48,* 1132-1140.

Index

AAAS. *See* African American Acculturation Scale
Abrahams, R. D., 6
Acceptable behaviors, 58, 60
Acceptance, of responsibility, 128,
135
Acculturated group:
from AAAS cluster analysis, 108
from AAAS median, 133
Acculturated individuals, 1-2
compared to traditional individuals.
See African American Acculturation Scale, studies
principle of return and, 53-56
social comparisons by, 58, 60
those most likely to become, 57
Acculturation:
as an acculturation model, 44
at the sociological level, 40-41
by social comparison, 58, 60

direction of, 43, 44, 45-46, 51,
53-56
importance of, as a concept, 2-3,
5, 8, 35
speed of, 56-57
Acculturation levels, 1-2, 41, 137
age and, 46, 53-54, 141
cigarette smoking and, 4-5, 90-96,
103-107, 110-112, 114, 116,
121, 124, 142
coping skills and, 132-136, 144
diabetes and, 143
education and, 137
foods and, 92, 97, 99, 118
hypertension and, 4, 96-100, 103,
112-114, 116, 125, 143
importance of, as a concept, 35
mental health and, 126-136,
143-144
mortality rates and, 143

About the Authors

Hope Landrine is an African American health and clinical psychologist. She received her Ph.D. in clinical psychology from the University of Rhode Island (1983). She did postdoctoral training in social psychology at Stanford University from 1984 to 1986, and in preventive medicine and cancer control as a National Cancer Institute Fellow, Department of Preventive Medicine, University of Southern California Medical School, from 1992 to 1993. She was a college professor for 7 years and is currently a Research Scientist at the Public Health Foundation (Los Angeles County), where she conducts full-time, grant-supported research and preventive interventions to improve the health of African American children and adults and of women and girls of all ethnic groups. She has published numerous articles on cultural diversity in preventive medicine and in feminist, health, and clinical psychology, and she received the 1994 APA MFP Achievement Award for

Outstanding Research on Cultural Diversity. Her other books include *The Politics of Madness* (1992), *Bringing Cultural Diversity to Feminist Psychology* (1995), and (with Elizabeth Klonoff) *Preventing Misdiagnosis of Women: A Guide to Physical Disorders With Psychiatric Symptoms* (in press).

Elizabeth A. Klonoff is a health and clinical psychologist who received her Ph.D. in clinical psychology from the University of Oregon in 1977. She taught in the Departments of Psychiatry, Pediatrics, Neurology, and Psychology at Case Western Reserve University Medical School and was Director of the Behavior Therapy Clinic at University Hospitals of Cleveland from 1979 to 1988. She has been teaching at California State University, San Bernardino (CSU-SB) since 1988, and she is currently a Professor of Psychology and Executive Director of the Behavioral Health Institute at CSU-SB. She has received over $1.3 million in grants to support her research on cultural diversity in clinical, health, and feminist psychology and on interventions to reduce tobacco use among African American children and adults. She has published numerous articles on cultural diversity and African American health. Her other books include (with Hope Landrine) *Preventing Misdiagnosis of Women: A Guide to Physical Disorders With Psychiatric Symptoms* (in press).